BEYOND

GRADES AND GOSSIPS

Volume – II:

Hearts & Hustle

Nilesh Kale

Title Verso

Title: Beyond Grades and Gossips

Publication: Author, Amazon Kindle

Year of Publication: April 2025

Edition: First – April 2025

Form of Book: E-Book Reader, Paper Back

Author: Nilesh S. Kale

Place of Publication: Belagavi (590 006), Karnataka, India.

ISBN for Print Version: 978-93-5890-107-8

Price: INR 100/- (For Kindle Version)

The characters, names and situations are purely hypothetical.

Author's Note

If Book One - ***'Beyond Grades and Gossips - Campus Crossroads'*** was a letter to every student who felt lost —

Book Two is a letter to every student who thought they had found themselves, and then discovered the finding was only just beginning.

Hearts & Hustle is the story of what happens after the first victory. After the dust settles. After everyone goes home for summer and comes back slightly different and pretends not to notice.

Love that grows quietly in library seats and chai tapri conversations. Dreams spoken out loud for the first time. Betrayal from unexpected directions. Standing for someone when standing costs you something.

A word about structure. Two chapters are numbered differently — 7B and 10B. Deliberately. Stories, like lives, do not unfold in perfect sequence. Sometimes something life-changing is happening in one room while everything else continues normally in another. These chapters exist in that space. A 7B sometimes arrives in the middle of everything. It does not wait for a convenient chapter number.

To every student who has ever sat in a corridor or a hostel terrace wondering if what they want is possible —

It is. You are seen.

— Nilesh Kale

Preface to Second Book in the Series:

Beyond Grades and Gossips: Hearts & Hustle

There is a confusion that does not arrive in the first year of anything.

It arrives later. After you know the corridors and the faces. After the first year's anxiety has been replaced by something that looks, from the outside, like confidence. The quiet voice that asks — *is this the life I am choosing, or simply the life happening to me?*

This is the confusion at the heart of Book Two.

Two new arrivals change everything without meaning to. Niel, who sees the truth in twelve words when everyone else needs two hundred. And Geet, who means well with her whole heart, creates chaos anyway, and turns out to be the most important witness in the room.

This book contains a theft. Someone takes Kabir's creative work and puts their name on it. What follows is not revenge. It is something cleaner. Evidence. Integrity. The courage of people who have learned that doing the right thing is always the right strategy.

The work lives in the maker. Not the submission portal.

Books Three, Four and Five are coming. The real world. The final battles. The full circle back to the same gate and the same amphitheater steps. Different people. Better people.

Look around when you finish. Your Venky Sir is probably closer than you think.

— Nilesh Kale

Table of Contents

Chapter 1: Same Gate, Different People:

The gate looked exactly the same.

Same rusted iron rods. Same faded white paint on the pillars. Same security guard who perpetually looked like he had better places to be. Same notice board just inside — sun-bleached, slightly crooked, plastered with flyers that nobody had actually read since 2019.

Aarav stood outside it, bag slung over one shoulder, and just — looked.

Three months had passed since graduation. Three months of summer heat, family pressure, confused career conversations at the dinner table, and too many evenings staring at the ceiling fan wondering what came next. And now here he was. Back at the same gate he had walked through a thousand times.

He had not expected it to feel like this.

Like coming home.

He took a breath. Adjusted his bag. And walked through.

The campus in late June was a different creature from the campus in March.

The Ganesh festival preparations hadn't started yet — that was still weeks away — but Pune had that particular pre-monsoon energy that made everything feel both restless and alive. The air smelled of wet earth and old paper and something fried from the canteen two buildings away.

Pigeons argued on the library roof. A group of new students stood near the admin block looking terrified in the specific way that only first days produce.

Aarav watched them for a moment.

That had been him once. Standing at that same notice board. Heart hammering. Not knowing a single soul.

He smiled quietly to himself and walked toward the amphitheater.

Kabir arrived forty minutes late.

This was, by Kabir's own standards, impressively early.

He appeared from the direction of the main road rather than the campus gate — which meant he had, once again, taken the wrong bus, gotten off at the wrong stop, and walked the remaining distance powered entirely by vada pav and optimism. He had a half-eaten vada pav in one hand, a bag that looked like it had been packed by someone mid-earthquake in the other, and an expression of complete serenity on his face.

"Aarav bhai." He dropped onto the amphitheater step beside him. "Miss me?"

"I've been here forty minutes."

"And what were you upto?"

"I was thinking." Arav said.

Kabir took a large bite of vada pav. "That's the same thing as wasting time, just with more suffering." He looked around at the campus with something genuinely soft in his eyes. "Same place. Feels different though, no?"

"Postgrad," Aarav said simply.

"Postgrad," Kabir agreed, as if the word explained everything about everything. Then, after a pause: "Do you think the canteen still has that terrible poha that somehow also tastes incredible?"

"Probably."

"Then life is good." He finished his vada pav and brushed his hands on his jeans. "Who else is coming?"

As if in answer, they heard footsteps — quick, precise, purposeful.

Sanya arrived with a new notebook. Teal. Spiral-bound. Already open to the first page which contained a colour-coded semester plan with three different highlighters.

Kabir stared at it. Then at her. Then back at it.

"You made a semester plan before the semester started."

"I made it three weeks ago," Sanya said, sitting down. "This is the revised version."

Kabir opened his mouth. Closed it. Then quietly said: "That's emotional damage."

Sanya gave him a look that was both withering and fond at the same time — a specific expression she had perfected over three years of sitting next to him. "Some of us like to be prepared."

"Some of us like to live."

"Some of us can do both."

Kabir pointed at her slowly. "That was good. I'll allow it."

Meera arrived last.

She came from the library side of campus — of course she did — walking with that particular unhurried pace she had, the one that always made it look like she had all the time in the world and was also somehow going somewhere important. Kurta, jeans, hair pulled back, a book tucked under one arm that she was clearly still reading as she walked.

She reached the amphitheater steps and looked up.

Aarav looked up at the same moment.

Their eyes met for exactly one second.

Something passed between them — quiet and unnamed and warm, like a door opening to a room you had almost forgotten existed. Then Meera looked at Kabir and smiled.

"You're on time for once."

"I'm forty minutes late."

"For you that's on time."

Kabir considered this with great seriousness. "Fair."

She sat down. The four of them were back together. Same steps. Same campus. Same Kabir reaching for someone else's snack without asking. But something in the air was gently, undeniably different. All four of them felt it.

None of them said so.

Some things change in a summer, even when nothing happens.

Rohan was already inside. Nobody had seen him arrive.

This was simply a Rohan thing. He existed in spaces before you noticed him entering them. He was at his usual spot — the windowsill near the water cooler on the second floor — reading something on his phone. He nodded once when the group passed.

"Hey," Aarav said.

"Hey," Rohan said.

This was, for them, a complete conversation.

Kabir waved at him with great enthusiasm. Rohan looked at the wave. Then at Kabir. Then back at his phone. Kabir counted this as a win.

It was Aarav who noticed him first.

They were heading toward the postgrad department corridor — old habits — when Aarav glanced to the far end of the hall and stopped walking.

Near the window where the afternoon light came in strongest, someone was sitting on the floor. Back against the wall. Long legs stretched out. Entirely at ease.

Reading.

Not on a phone. An actual book — thick, dog-eared at several points — held with the kind of relaxed focus that made it clear this was not performance. This was simply what he did while he waited.

Around him the corridor was full chaos. New students dragging luggage. Someone arguing with a clerk about a form. A group of seniors laughing loudly. The general beautiful mayhem of the first day of a new year.

He was in the middle of all of it.

Completely unbothered by any of it.

"Who's that?" Meera asked quietly, following Aarav's gaze.

"No idea," Aarav said.

The person turned a page.

"New student?" Kabir squinted.

"Must be."

"He's reading in a corridor on the first day," Sanya said. There was something unmistakably approving in her voice.

As if sensing the attention — or perhaps simply reaching the end of a chapter — the person looked up. He scanned the corridor with calm, unhurried eyes. His gaze moved across the chaos without any particular reaction, taking it all in quietly. And then, briefly, it landed on the four of them watching him from twenty feet away.

He didn't smile. Didn't wave. Didn't look away awkwardly either.

He gave the smallest, most composed nod — the kind that said I see you, I'm not performing anything for you, we can talk when there's a reason to talk — and looked back down at his book.

"Interesting," Kabir said.

Aarav said nothing. But he kept thinking about those eyes — the quality of stillness in them. The way they had taken in the entire corridor without being pulled around by any of it.

He had never met this person. He already felt like he had encountered this person before, in a book, in a story someone once told him about what it looked like when a person was genuinely comfortable in their own skin.

At three-thirty, Professor Venkatesh Krishnamurthy (Venky Sir) came around the corner.

Same blazer. Artfully unbuttoned, as always. Same chai cup — not the same physical cup obviously, but one that had clearly been chosen as the spiritual successor to every chai cup that came before it. He walked at the precise pace of a man who was never in a hurry because he was always exactly where he needed to be.

He turned the corner. Saw them. Stopped.

He looked at the four of them — standing in the postgrad corridor in their slightly uncertain, slightly excited, first-day-of-a-new-chapter state — and something in his expression changed. Not a smile exactly. Something quieter and warmer. The look of someone who has watched a good story unfold and is quietly pleased to see where it goes next.

He raised his chai cup in their direction.

Not a word. Just that. Then he walked on.

The four of them stood there watching him go.

"He didn't even say anything," Meera said softly.

"He didn't need to," Aarav said.

And somehow — after the confusion and the heat and the unnamed something in the air and everything that three months of summer had quietly rearranged inside each of them — that single raised cup of chai felt like the most grounding thing that had happened all day.

They were back.

The real work was about to begin.

Chapter 2: The New Equation

Orientation for postgraduate students was held in Seminar Hall B — which was slightly smaller than Seminar Hall A and significantly less well air-conditioned, a fact the administration appeared to be entirely at peace with.

Forty-two students filed in. Some knew each other from undergrad. Some were entirely new — transfers from other colleges, a couple from other cities. The room had that particular first-day energy: everyone quietly assessing everyone else, nobody admitting to it.

Aarav, Meera, Kabir, and Sanya found four seats together near the middle. Rohan slipped in and sat two rows behind — close enough to be part of them, far enough to be apart. Classic Rohan geometry.

The new professor, Dr. Pramod Joshi — young, eager, the type who had clearly prepared extensively for this orientation — began speaking about the postgraduate curriculum, the expectations, the opportunities.

Three minutes in, Kabir leaned toward Aarav and whispered: "He said 'synergy'. Drink."

"We're not drinking anything."

"Mentally drink."

Dr. Joshi said "leverage" and "holistic development" within the same sentence.

Kabir silently keeled over sideways. Aarav pushed him back upright.

She walked into the wrong classroom.

That was how Geet entered their lives — not through a door she meant to open, but through one she opened completely by accident with the full confidence of someone who had absolutely no reason to doubt herself.

She stood at the front of Seminar Hall B, dupatta slightly askew, a bag shaped like a sunflower over one shoulder, looking at forty-two faces looking back at her.

"Is this..." she checked something on her phone. Looked up. Looked at the board behind Dr. Joshi that clearly said POSTGRADUATE ORIENTATION — M.COM BATCH. Looked back at her phone. "Oh."

A pause.

"This is not the library."

Silence.

Then, from somewhere in the middle of the room, a laugh escaped. One genuine laugh. And then the whole room followed because the laugh had been so spontaneous and so real that nobody could help it.

Geet looked at the laughing room with an expression of great dignity.

"I meant to do that," she said. "It's an icebreaker. You're all very welcome."

More laughter. Dr. Joshi tried to look strict and failed.

"Actually," she said, "is this the M.Com postgrad? Because I might be in the right place for the wrong reasons."

Dr. Joshi checked his list. "Name?"

"Geet Sharma."

He found her. "You're in the right room. Sit down, please."

Geet scanned the room for a seat. Her eyes landed on the empty chair next to Sanya. She walked over, settled in with the ease of someone arriving at a place they had always intended to be, and put her sunflower bag on her lap.

"Hi," she whispered to Sanya. "I actually wasn't lost. I came from the floor above by mistake but I knew what floor I needed once I saw the sign. The confidence is real."

Sanya stared at her.

"I'm Geet."

"Sanya."

"Do you have a colour-coded notebook?"

"...Yes."

Geet's eyes lit up. "Oh, we are going to be friends."

Niel was introduced to them by Kabir.

This was perhaps the most Kabir way for anything to happen. Kabir simply talked to everyone — it was less a social choice and more a natural phenomenon, like weather. You did not question why it rained. You simply got wet.

They were at the chai tapri (small retail shop that particularly serves tea with small snacks) outside the postgrad block after orientation. The five of them plus Geet, who had attached herself to Sanya with the quiet determination of a very sincere sticker.

Kabir spotted Niel at the far end of the tapri — same person from the corridor, same book, now with a cutting chai — and walked over before anyone could say anything.

"Bhai, you're new here?"

Niel looked up from his book. Took in Kabir's expression — open, energetic, genuinely curious — and seemed to make an assessment.

"Transferred from Nashik," he said.

"M.Com?"

"Yes."

"Then we're batch-mates." Kabir gestured broadly at the group. "Come sit. We don't bite. Except Sanya but only during exam season."

Sanya, from six feet away: "I can hear you."

"I know," Kabir said serenely.

Niel picked up his chai and his book and came over. He sat. He looked at the group — all six faces now watching him — and said nothing. Not awkwardly. Just without any need to fill the silence.

Kabir introduced everyone. Niel nodded at each name with that same quality of genuine, unhurried attention.

Then Kabir said, "So what's the book?"

Niel held it up. *Thinking, Fast and Slow* by Daniel Kahneman.

"Is it good?" Kabir asked.

"It explains why people make the same mistakes repeatedly and believe they won't."

"Brutal," Kabir said.

"Accurate," Niel said.

Kabir grinned. He liked this person immediately and with complete certainty. Kabir's gut was rarely wrong about people.

Aarav watched the exchange. Something about the way Niel had said *accurate* — not with arrogance, just with the calm matter-of-factness of someone stating a thing they had genuinely thought about — made him feel a particular kind of curiosity. The kind you feel around people who are different in a way you cannot immediately name.

Meera, sitting across, caught Aarav's expression. She raised an eyebrow slightly. He shrugged slightly back. One of those wordless micro-conversations they had been having for years without ever acknowledging that they had them.

Geet, who had been listening, said to Niel: "Is there a chapter about accidentally going to the wrong classroom?"

Niel considered this seriously. "Chapter four. The planning fallacy."

Geet pointed at him. "I like you."

That evening, the new group of six settled naturally into what would become their spot — the left side of the amphitheater, third step from the bottom. Rohan drifted over eventually and sat at the end without being asked, the way he always did.

The campus was quieter now. The golden Pune evening light was doing its best work. Somewhere from the FC Road direction came the faint smell of street food and petrol and the general wonderful chaos of the city going about its life.

Kabir had somehow acquired six cutting chais from the tapri and was distributing them with the generosity of someone who had spent other people's money.

"New year," he said, lifting his chai like a toast. "New chapter."

"Same people making the same mistakes," Sanya said.

"Speak for yourself," Kabir said.

"I am speaking for you."

Geet lifted her chai very seriously. "I'm new here so I don't know what the mistakes are yet. But I'll make my own. Possibly starting tomorrow."

Niel drank his chai without comment. But there was something at the corner of his mouth that wasn't quite a smile and wasn't quite not one.

Aarav sat back and looked at the sky going orange above the campus roofline. He thought about the gate this morning. The notice board. That moment of standing outside and feeling like something was beginning.

He was right. Something was.

He just didn't know yet that most of it had nothing to do with coursework.

Three rows behind the group, Venky Sir stood at the department corridor window on the second floor, chai in hand, looking down at the amphitheater.

He could see them from here. All seven of them — the old four, the quiet grey shape that was Rohan, and the two new faces.

He watched for a moment. Then he looked specifically at Niel — that calm, reading-in-corridors, *accurate* kind of person — and something moved in his expression that was harder to name. Something old. Something that had nothing to do with today.

He took a slow sip of chai.

Some students you teach, he thought. Some students you recognize.

He turned from the window and went back to his desk.

Chapter 3: FC Road and Other Confusions

FC Road on a Pune evening is not just a road.

It is an experience. A state of mind. A place where college students have been having the same conversations about love and ambition and the price of vada pav for forty years, and where every conversation feels like the first time anyone has ever had it.

The group arrived on Friday evening — all six of them, plus Geet who had invited herself with the simple confidence of someone who assumed she was always included until told otherwise. Nobody had told her otherwise.

Kabir led the way with the authority of a man who had walked this road many times and still managed to find new things to argue about on it. Sanya had her notebook. Geet had a tote bag that said *I READ BOOKS AND I KNOW THINGS* which was only partly accurate. Niel had, naturally, a book.

"You cannot bring a book to FC Road," Kabir told him.

"I brought a book."

"You cannot."

"I did."

Kabir turned to the group. "Is anyone going to tell him?"

"Let him live," Meera said.

Kabir pointed at Niel. "She has protected you today. Remember this."

Niel tucked the book into his bag without expression.

"He did it," Aarav observed.

"Because it was logical," Niel said. "Not because Kabir told me to."

Kabir threw his arm around Niel's shoulders. "I love this guy. He's like a fortune cookie that argues back."

They settled at their usual spot — the low wall outside the old bookshop that had no name written on it anymore because the letters had faded and the owner had decided mystery was good for business.

Chai arrived. Then vada pav. Then more chai because chai on FC Road is not an event, it is a continuum.

Aarav and Meera ended up walking slightly behind the rest of the group at some point — not by design, simply by the natural drift of a conversation that had wandered away from the group and into its own territory.

They were talking about nothing important.

Which meant they were talking about everything important.

"Did you think you'd come back?" Meera asked. She was looking ahead at the road, not at him.

"For postgrad?"

"Yes."

Aarav thought about it honestly. "Part of me wanted to just — go. Get a job, figure out the real world. But I kept feeling like I wasn't done here yet." He paused. "Which sounds strange."

"It doesn't," she said immediately. Then, after a moment: "I almost didn't come back."

Aarav stopped walking.

He caught himself. Kept walking. But something had shifted — a small internal movement, like something that had been sitting still suddenly turning to face a direction.

"Why?" he asked.

Meera was quiet for a beat. "I got an offer. A company in Mumbai. Not a big one. But real work, you know? Not campus."

"What happened?"

"I said no." She finally glanced at him. "I'm not entirely sure why."

Aarav held that. Turned it over. Said nothing.

Why does it matter that she almost didn't come back? Why does the image of this campus without her in it feel so specifically wrong?

He didn't analyse it. He just felt it and let it pass and kept walking.

Meera was already talking about something else.

The bookshop chaos happened thirty minutes later.

Geet had wandered in to browse while the group waited outside. This was the first mistake. The second mistake was nobody designating a responsible adult to accompany her.

The sound from inside the shop began as a small clatter. Then a louder one. Then the bookshop owner's voice — old man, famously particular about his collection — rising sharply.

They all looked at the shop.

Geet appeared in the doorway holding a chai glass that was now empty, wearing an expression of profound apology.

"I was gesturing while explaining something," she said, "and the chai went — it kind of — there was a shelf of first editions."

The bookshop owner appeared behind her, looking the way people look when something they love has been irreversibly harmed.

What followed was a ten-minute event.

Kabir went in to negotiate — with the air of a diplomat arriving at a conflict he hadn't caused but was constitutionally obligated to fix. He used words like "unfortunate accident" and "the sincerity of her regret" and "chai can be cleaned, sir, but your collection is priceless."

Sanya went in to apologise formally and specifically, which she did with a prepared sincerity that momentarily surprised the owner into listening.

Geet stood to the side being genuinely horrified by herself in the specific way that made it impossible to stay angry at her.

And Niel quietly walked in, asked the owner which books had been affected, calculated the cost of professional cleaning versus replacement, and placed the money on the counter without drama or announcement.

By the time anyone noticed what he had done, Niel was already back outside looking at the road.

"You paid for it?" Aarav asked him.

"It was the fastest solution," Niel said simply.

Inside, the owner was now laughing — genuinely, warmly — at something Kabir had said. The crisis was over.

Kabir came out looking satisfied. "I handled that beautifully."

Sanya looked at Niel. Niel said nothing.

"He paid," Meera told Kabir.

Kabir looked at Niel. Niel was watching the traffic on FC Road.

"Bhai," Kabir said quietly.

"Don't," Niel said.

Kabir looked at him for a long moment. Then he put his hand on Niel's shoulder very briefly and said nothing more.

That was the moment Kabir went from liking Niel to trusting him. Not because he paid. Because he hadn't wanted anyone to notice that he paid.

Geet, in the aftermath, sat on the wall next to Sanya with the expression of someone conducting a serious internal review.

"I create chaos," she said.

"Yes," Sanya agreed.

"But I don't mean to."

"I know."

"Does that make it better or worse?"

Sanya thought about it. "Better for your character. Worse for the people around you."

Geet considered this. "That's honest."

"You asked."

Geet nodded slowly, then said: "I'm going to buy that owner a plant tomorrow. As an apology gift. Plants are healing."

"That's a good idea."

"I'll put it in a pot that says *sorry for the chai* on it."

"That might be too much."

"Or exactly enough?"

Sanya opened her notebook and wrote something. Geet looked at it. It said: *Geet — high chaos, high intention, genuinely good person.* She had drawn a small star next to it.

Geet stared at it for a moment. Then she very quietly said: "Nobody has written something nice about me in a notebook before."

Sanya looked at her. "Get used to it."

The evening ended late. The kind of late that happens when nobody wants to be the first to say it's time to go.

They were back on the low wall, the whole group, the city humming around them. Kabir was doing an impression of Dr. Joshi saying *synergy* that was becoming more accurate with each repetition. Meera was laughing so hard she had put her head on Sanya's shoulder. Geet was contributing additional *synergy* sound effects. Rohan was at the edge of the group — almost smiling.

Aarav stayed back a little at the chai tapri on the way out, waiting for the last round.

Niel stayed back too. Not by coordination. Just because he wasn't in a rush.

They stood there for a moment in a comfortable silence. Two people who barely knew each other, equally unbothered by the quiet.

Then Aarav said: "Why'd you transfer from Nashik?"

Niel looked at the road. "The programme here is better."

"Just that?"

A pause. "And I wanted to be in a place where things happened." He glanced at Aarav. "People said interesting things happen at this college."

Aarav thought about the last year. The placement scam. The election. The protests. Venky Sir.

"They do," he said.

"Good," Niel said.

Aarav slowed near the gate instead of immediately catching up with the others.

The FC Road noise had softened slightly behind them. Somewhere nearby, someone was arguing passionately about cricket. A bike sped past. Pune continued being Pune.

“Do you ever feel,” Aarav said suddenly, “like everyone else already knows who they’re becoming?”

Niel glanced at him but didn’t interrupt.

Aarav laughed softly at himself.

“Kabir knows what he loves. Sanya acts like she has a backup plan for her backup plan. Meera...” He paused briefly. “Meera walks like she already has a destination.”

“And you?” Niel asked.

"I think I just react faster than I panic."

That earned the smallest smile from Niel.

"Most people aren't lost because they don't have direction," he said quietly. "They're lost because they think everyone else does."

The silence after that didn't feel awkward.

It felt understood.

They walked back to the group.

It was a small conversation. But Aarav had the feeling — the specific, quiet kind — that this person was going to matter. He couldn't say why yet. He just knew.

Some things you know before you have the evidence.

They walked back toward the gate.

It was Kabir who spotted the camera sign-out sheet on the way back.

They were cutting through the media block — shorter route to the gate, Kabir's discovery, third week of semester. The sheet was pinned to the lab door the way all important things were pinned on this campus — slightly crooked, slightly ignored.

Kabir stopped. Read it.

Both cameras. The entire coming weekend. One name.

Vikram Nair.

He stood there for a moment. Then he took out his phone and booked the only remaining slot — Tuesday evening, three hours, the small camera not the good one.

"You, okay?" Meera asked.

"Fine," Kabir said. Already walking. "Just planning something."

He did not explain what.

He had learned, somewhere along the way, that the things worth doing were best kept quiet until they were done.

The disaster happened three days later.

Which, according to Sanya, was approximately three days longer than statistically expected with Geet involved.

The group had been preparing material for the inter-college innovation fellowship presentation — slides, notes, rough strategy documents, all living temporarily inside a shared drive that Sanya guarded with the emotional intensity of national security.

Geet froze midway through the discussion.

“I think,” she said slowly, staring at her phone, “I may have sent the draft presentation to the wrong group.”

Nobody reacted immediately.

Kabir blinked once. “Wrong group meaning?”

Geet swallowed.

“The inter-college coordination group.”

Silence. Sanya snatched the phone from her hand.

“Oh excellent,” she said flatly. “You accidentally shared our incomplete strategy with every competing college.”

“I said sorry already!”

“You said ‘oops,’ Geet. That is not an apology. That is a sound effect.”

Even Aarav looked stressed now.

Only Niel stayed calm.

“How bad is it?” he asked.

Sanya kept scrolling. “...bad enough.”

Geet sat down slowly, guilt visibly crushing her usual awkward energy.

Kabir quietly placed a water bottle beside her.

“We’ll handle it,” he said simply.

She nodded without looking at anyone.

At the far edge of the corridor, Rohan — who had been unusually silent through the entire discussion — looked at the forwarded file name for one second too long.

Nobody noticed.

Chapter 4: What Meera Doesn't Say

She had started writing it on the fifteenth of July.

Not a diary exactly. She had never been a diary person — diaries implied a constant narrator, and Meera's inner life was less a running commentary and more a series of photographs, moments she wanted to hold still and look at properly.

So, she wrote things down. Observations. Questions. Sometimes just a single word that was trying to mean more than it could say.

On the fifteenth of July, in the third week of the postgrad semester, she wrote:

Why does a good day feel better when Kabir makes it funny?

She did not think much of it. Kabir made everyone's days funnier. That was simply his function in the universe.

Three days later she wrote:

He remembered I don't like too much sugar in my chai. He just handed me the right one without asking.

She looked at this sentence for a long time after writing it.

Then she told herself it meant nothing and went to sleep.

Here is what was actually happening, though Meera would not have used this language at the time:

She was confused.

Not in a dramatic, film-song way. In a quiet, Tuesday-afternoon, sitting-in-the-library way. The slow kind of confusion that builds when you have been through something difficult — the Rohan situation, the breakup, the months of feeling slightly off-centre — and then slowly come back to yourself, and in the process of coming back you find that some furniture has been rearranged.

She knew what she had felt with Rohan. She knew what that had been — real at first, then complicated, then small in a way that felt wrong.

But now? These feelings were different. Lighter. Safer. Kabir made her laugh like nobody could. He always knew when she was low before she said so. He handed her the right chai without asking.

She was twenty-two years old and smart in most directions. But the heart has its own curriculum and it does not follow the syllabus.

Sanya noticed.

Of course, Sanya noticed. Sanya noticed everything and said nothing until she had decided what to say, which meant she was always three observations ahead of the conversation.

She noticed the way Meera's eyes followed Kabir when he was being particularly himself. The slight smile that appeared on Meera's face a half-second before the laugh. The way Meera mentioned Kabir in conversations that had nothing to do with Kabir.

She said nothing for two weeks.

She filed it carefully in that organized mind of hers, like a document she wasn't ready to open yet.

And she watched.

The project happened in the fourth week.

Their postgrad Business Communication professor, Dr. Anjali Desai — efficient, direct, and constitutionally allergic to nonsense — assigned project pairs for a semester-long presentation. She called the names herself.

"Aarav Kapoor and Meera Nair."

Meera looked at Aarav across the room.

Aarav looked at Meera.

Neither of them said anything.

Kabir, sitting behind Aarav, poked him in the back. Aarav did not turn around.

The library became their workspace. Tuesday and Thursday evenings, eight to ten, second floor near the window because

Meera always chose the window seat and Aarav had long since stopped arguing about it.

It was not complicated at first. They were good at working together — had been for three years. They divided tasks efficiently. They argued about approach in the specific way where both people are right about different things and neither wants to admit it. They made it work.

But late evenings in libraries have their own quality. The lights go a little softer. The campus outside quietens. People begin talking in the register reserved for actual things rather than academic things.

And slowly, without either of them noticing the shift, they stopped working and started talking.

About the summer. About what they had each been afraid of, coming back. About the strange sensation of being in a place you know well but feeling like a new version of yourself inside it.

On Thursday of the third week, Aarav fell asleep.

Not dramatically. Not in the middle of a sentence. He had been reading something, and at some point, between one paragraph and the next, his head dropped to his folded arms on the table and the reading simply stopped.

Meera looked at him for a moment.

Then she looked around the library. Empty. Just them and the quiet.

She reached into her bag and took out her dupatta — the light cotton one she always carried — and placed it carefully around his shoulders.

He didn't wake up.

She sat back down and looked at him — at the way his shoulders rose and fell, at the library light falling across his face — for a moment that was longer than a moment.

She didn't know what she was feeling exactly.

She just knew it was something.

She opened her notebook and looked at the page she had been writing on.

Without thinking about it, she wrote a word.

One word. In the margin. Small.

Then she closed the notebook quickly and went back to her reading.

The chaos of that week came, as it always did, through Geet.

She had meant to send a voice note to Sanya. She had pressed the wrong name in her contacts. The voice note went, instead, to the entire class group chat.

The voice note was forty-seven seconds long.

In it, Geet could be heard singing — with feeling and some talent — a filmy sad song from a nineties film about unrequited love. Then, at the end, in a completely normal speaking voice: "Okay Sanya, I was obviously singing that for the CHARACTER in the story I'm writing, not for any real reason. Just to be clear. Anyway, what time is the library closing today?"

The class group chat exploded.

By morning, seventeen people had saved the voice note. Four had made it their ringtone. One person — nobody could identify who — had set it as the hold music for the student council helpline.

Kabir saved it within twelve seconds of it being sent. He labelled it in his phone:

GEET_MASTERPIECE_DO_NOT_DELETE.

Geet, in response to the chaos, wrote in the group: The character's name is Priya and she is going through a very hard time and deserves your sympathy.

Sanya showed up at Geet's door that evening.

"Which character?" she asked.

"Priya," Geet said.

"Is Priya you?"

A pause. "Priya is entirely fictional."

"Geeeet???"

"...Priya is mostly fictional."

Sanya sat down. "Tell me about Priya."

Geet sat down across from her. And then, because Geet was the kind of person who found it impossible to be dishonest when someone was being genuinely kind to her, she told her.

It was not about Priya.

Meera went to Venky Sir's office on a Wednesday.

She went officially for academic guidance. She had questions about a research methodology paper. This was entirely true.

Venky Sir answered the research methodology questions in exactly eight minutes — efficiently, clearly, with two additional references she hadn't asked for but would find useful.

And waited.

Meera looked at the papers in front of her. "Sir, I had one more thing."

"Of course you did," he said. Not unkindly.

"Hypothetically."

"Always a good start."

"If someone is — " she chose the words carefully. "If someone is confused about what they feel toward a person, and they can't tell if it's something real or just — comfort. Familiarity. Is there a way to know?"

Venky Sir was quiet for a moment.

He set his chai down.

"Don't ask your heart," he said. "The heart performs for an audience. Ask your habits instead."

Meera looked at him.

"Who do you think about when something good happens?" he said. "Not when you're sad — that tells you who you run to for safety, which is different. When something genuinely good happens — a small victory, a piece of news that makes you happy — who is the first person you want to tell?"

The office was very quiet.

Outside, the campus went about its evening.

Meera thought about the answer to that question.

She thought about it carefully and honestly. The question had the answer for her.

And then she stood up, gathered her papers, thanked him for the research guidance, and left.

Venky Sir watched the door close.

He took a long sip of chai.

These things always sort themselves, he thought. They just need time and a good question.

That night, Meera sat at her desk in her hostel room.

She opened her notebook to the margin where she had written the word.

She looked at it for a long time.

Then she did not cross it out.

She turned the page and wrote a question.

Who do I want to tell first?

She sat with it. The room was quiet. Her roommate was asleep. Somewhere outside a night bird was doing its best.

The answer came without drama. Without fanfare. Without a background score.

It came the way true things tend to come — quietly, clearly, having been there for a while already.

She closed the notebook.

She did not open it again that night.

But she was smiling.

Chapter 5: The Niel Effect

There is a particular kind of person who changes the temperature of a room without trying to.

Not the loud kind. Not the kind who walks in and demands attention with volume or charm or the social equivalent of a foghorn. That kind is common enough. You find them at every orientation, every fresher's party, every group project that somehow becomes about one person.

No. The rarer kind is quieter. They walk in, find a wall to lean against, and simply — exist. With such complete comfort in their own existence that the people around them slowly start to wonder what it would feel like to be that settled inside themselves.

Niel was that kind.

By the end of the third week, the group had all felt it independently and in their own way. None of them had named it yet.

The first thing Niel did that made the group pay attention — really pay attention — happened on a Monday morning.

Dr. Arvind Kulkarni was a professor of the old school variety. Not old school in the charming, wise, tough-but-fair way. Old school in the way that meant he had been teaching the same notes from the same yellowed pages for eleven years and considered any question that deviated from those notes to be a personal challenge to his authority.

He was mid-lecture on organizational behaviour when a student — second row, quiet, the kind of student who always sat in the second row and was always quiet — raised his hand and asked a question.

It was a good question. A genuinely curious one. The kind that comes from someone actually thinking about the material rather than just writing it down.

Dr. Kulkarni paused. Looked at the student. And said, with the measured coldness of someone who had perfected this particular weapon over eleven years:

"If you had been paying attention instead of waiting for your moment to speak, you would know that I addressed this in the previous class. Kindly revise your notes before asking questions that waste everyone's time."

The student went red. The class went quiet in the specific uncomfortable way of forty people collectively deciding not to make eye contact with anyone.

Dr. Kulkarni returned to his yellowed pages.

Three seconds of silence.

Then Niel raised his hand.

Dr. Kulkarni looked at him. He had noticed Niel — the transferred student, the one who read books in corridors, the one whose assignments were returned without a single correction mark. He looked at him now with the particular expression reserved for people you cannot easily dismiss.

"Yes?"

"Sir," Niel said. His voice was entirely calm. Not confrontational. Not performing bravery for an audience. Just calm. "The question Rahul asked — I checked the previous class notes last night. That specific aspect of psychological safety in organizational structures wasn't addressed. He was right to ask."

A pause.

"Are you suggesting I don't know my own curriculum?"

"I'm suggesting there might be a gap worth filling," Niel said. "The question was good. The topic is relevant to three of the semester's assessment objectives." He placed his notes on the desk with the quiet finality of someone who had done the work. "I can share the page references if that helps."

The classroom had stopped breathing.

Dr. Kulkarni looked at Niel for a long moment.

Then he looked at his notes.

Then, in the way of a man recalibrating without wishing to appear to recalibrate, he said: "We will address it in the next session," and returned to his lecture.

The student in the second row — Rahul — stared at the back of Niel's head.

Aarav, three seats away, stared at the side of Niel's face.

Niel had already returned to writing notes. As if the previous ninety seconds had been a small and unremarkable administrative matter.

After class, in the corridor, Kabir grabbed Niel's arm.

"Brother," he said. "That was — " He searched for the word. "That was something."

"Someone needed to say it," Niel said.

"Most people don't say it."

"I know."

"Doesn't that bother you? That most people don't say it?"

Niel thought about this for a genuine moment. "It used to," he said. "Now I just — say it, when it needs saying, and move on."

Kabir stared at him.

"What?" Niel said.

"Nothing," Kabir said. "I'm just deciding if you're real."

The second thing happened quietly, without audience.

Kabir had been struggling with the research methodology assignment. Not catastrophically — Kabir was sharper than most people gave him credit for, including occasionally himself — but he had hit a particular wall. A conceptual one. The kind where you can see the shape of the answer but cannot find the door to it.

He hadn't told anyone. Kabir had a very specific relationship with asking for help — he could offer it endlessly and receive it reluctantly, which is a common condition and an exhausting one.

He came to the library table one morning to find his textbook already open to the relevant chapter. A page of handwritten notes sat on top of it. At the top, in clean handwriting:

Different angle. Same answer.

That was all.

No name. No annotation. No performance of generosity.

Kabir sat down and read the notes.

They were clear. Precise. They approached the problem from a direction Kabir hadn't considered, and within twenty minutes he had not only solved his immediate problem but understood the underlying concept well enough to explain it to someone else.

He looked around the library. Niel was at a table three rows away, reading. He did not look up.

Kabir looked at the notes again.

He thought about saying something. He decided against it. He put the notes in his bag and opened his assignment.

Two days later, Kabir left a vada pav on Niel's library desk with a small note that said: *For services rendered. No need to acknowledge. We are even.*

Niel found it. Read the note. Looked across the library at Kabir, who was studiously looking at his book.

Niel ate the vada pav.

Neither of them ever spoke about it.

This was the correct response and both of them knew it.

The third thing was the one everyone saw.

It was a Thursday afternoon, the kind that Pune does particularly well — clouds building over the Western Ghats, a pre-rain coolness in the air, the campus slowing to that pleasant late-afternoon pace.

Niel and Venky Sir met properly for the first time.

Not in a classroom. In the corridor outside the postgrad staffroom, where Venky Sir was standing at the window with his chai, looking at the sky with the expression of a man conducting an unhurried conversation with the weather.

Niel was passing. He slowed. Looked at the same sky.

"Rain tonight?" he said.

Venky Sir glanced at him. This was not the first time a student had made small talk with him in corridors — students were always trying to make small talk with him, usually for strategic reasons involving marks or recommendations or the hope that proximity to wisdom was somehow transferable. He could tell the difference between that kind of small talk and the genuine kind within about four seconds.

He looked at Niel.

"Rain tomorrow morning," he said. "Tonight is just the warning."

As Niel shifted slightly against the windowsill, his eyes drifted toward the half-open cabin door behind Venky Sir.

Inside, on the desk near the lamp, an old photograph rested partly inside a book.

A younger Venky.

No beard. Bigger smile.

And beside him, a woman Niel had never seen before.

Simple cotton saree. Soft expression. The kind of smile that looked completely unaware of itself.

Venky noticed where Niel's eyes had moved.

Without urgency, he stepped inside, turned the photograph face-down beside the book, and returned to the corridor.

For a brief second, neither of them spoke.

Then Venky took another sip of chai.

“Some memories don't disturb you anymore,” he said quietly.

“They just sit with you.”

Niel considered this. "The sky performs before it commits."

Venky Sir was quiet for exactly one beat.

Then he said: "Sit down."

There was no chair. Niel sat on the windowsill across from him. Venky Sir leaned against the opposite wall. Between them, the corridor went about its business.

What followed lasted forty minutes. Nobody timed it — Rohan happened to pass the corridor twice during this period and clocked it on instinct, the way he clocked most things, silently and without comment.

Nobody knew what they talked about. Aarav asked Niel later, casually, trying not to seem like he was asking.

"Everything," Niel said.

"Like what?"

"Leadership. Mistakes. What makes a question good. Why most people answer the question they wish they'd been asked instead of the one they were actually asked." He paused. "Tea versus chai."

"Tea versus chai?"

"He has opinions."

Aarav laughed. “Did he psychologically analyse you too?”

“Probably,” Niel said.

“You seem weirdly calm about that.”

Niel adjusted the file in his hand slightly.

“Sleep deprivation reduces emotional resistance,” he said dryly.

Aarav looked at him properly then.

“You’re not sleeping?”

Niel gave a small shrug.

“Productively avoiding the question.”

Aarav smiled. "What did you think of him?"

Niel looked at the road ahead of them for a moment. When he answered, it was without performance or decoration.

"I think," he said, "that he is the kind of teacher that only happens once, if you're lucky."

Aarav told Venky Sir about the conversation with Niel two days later. He didn't plan to — it came out during one of those unplanned corridor stops that somehow always turned into real conversations with Venky Sir.

Venky Sir listened. Drank his chai.

"What do you think of him?" Aarav asked.

Venky Sir was quiet for a moment. He looked out the window at the campus below — at the students crossing the courtyard, at the pigeons, at the chai tapri sending up its constant small ribbon of steam.

"Some students," he said, "you teach."

A pause.

"Some students," he continued, "you recognize."

He didn't explain the distinction.

He didn't need to.

"And in some students, you see yourself."

The library stayed open late during postgrad season because nobody trusted postgrad students to maintain healthy schedules voluntarily.

By eleven-thirty, the reading hall had thinned out almost completely.

Kabir had fallen asleep over his notes twenty minutes ago. Geet was pretending to study while secretly doodling dramatic flowers in the margin of her notebook. Aarav had left after loudly declaring academic systems unconstitutional.

But Meera was still working.

Not absentmindedly.

Focused.

The kind of focus that made the rest of the room feel slower.

Sanya closed her notebook and watched her for a moment.

“You don’t stop, do you?”

Meera looked up briefly. “I do.”

“When?”

A small pause.

“After I become the version of myself, I’ll respect.”

For once, Sanya had no immediate reply ready.

She just looked at Meera differently after that.

Meanwhile, in the parallel universe of Meera's emotional life, the confusion was reaching a gentle crisis point.

She had not written the word again. She had not crossed it out either. The notebook sat on her desk every evening like a question she had asked herself and had not yet fully answered.

Here is what she knew:

She liked being around Kabir. She felt safe with him. She laughed with him the way she laughed with nobody else — the kind of laughter that comes from somewhere below the chest, from the part of you that has completely let its guard down.

And she liked being around Aarav. She felt — what was the word. Seen, maybe. Not in the performative way. In the specific way of someone who notices the things you don't announce. Who remembers you don't like too much sugar. Who falls asleep at a library table and trusts you enough to let that happen.

Kabir was aware of the sugar-likings of all the members of the group. Meera thought Kabir only remembers her choices. The dramatic chaos in the brain of Meera was real.

The problem, which she was beginning to suspect was not a problem but an answer in disguise, was this:

When Kabir made her laugh — she wanted to look at Aarav to see if he was laughing too.

Every time. Without fail.

Happiness, apparently, had a direction.

She went to the amphitheater on a Sunday afternoon when it was empty.

Just her and the steps and the Pune sky doing its complicated things overhead.

She opened the notebook.

She read the word in the margin.

Aarav.

She read Venky Sir's question.

Who do you think about when something good happens?

She sat with it.

And then, because she was Meera and she had always been more honest with herself than was strictly comfortable, she stopped pretending she didn't already know.

She did know.

She had known for a while.

She was not in love with Kabir. She loved Kabir the way you love someone who has been good to you in one of the hardest years of your life — completely, gratefully, without any requirement for it to be anything other than what it was. The love of deep friendship. The kind that doesn't need a definition and doesn't suffer from not having one.

What she felt about Aarav was different.

Different in the way that certain things are different — not louder, not more dramatic, but operating at a different frequency. The kind you feel in your habits rather than your headlines.

She closed the notebook.

She looked at the empty amphitheater around her.

"Okay," she said to nobody.

Then she went back to her room and did not do anything about it, because knowing something and doing something about it are two entirely separate departments, and the second department requires a kind of courage the first department does not issue automatically.

Sanya found her that evening.

She knocked, came in, sat on the edge of the bed, and looked at Meera with that specific expression she had — the one that said *I already know, I've known for a while, I was waiting for you to catch up.*

"Stop," Meera said.

"I haven't said anything."

"You're making the face."

"I don't have a face."

"Sanya. You have a very specific face."

Sanya folded her hands in her lap. "How long?"

Meera looked at the ceiling. "I don't know."

"How long do you think?"

A pause. "A while."

"And Kabir?"

Meera was quiet for a moment. Then: "That was never — it was never what I thought it was. It was just. He made the last year survivable. I confused gratitude for something else."

Sanya nodded slowly.

"Does that make me terrible?"

"No," Sanya said. "It makes you human. Feelings mislabel themselves all the time. The decent thing is noticing when they do."

Meera looked at her. "When did you know? About Kabir, I mean. That it wasn't—"

"The day you told me about the dupatta," Sanya said simply.

Meera stared. "I didn't tell you about the dupatta."

"You didn't have to."

"How did you—"

"You had chai with me the morning after. You talked about the library project for eleven minutes. You described the light in the library. You described what Aarav looked like asleep." Sanya raised an eyebrow. "You described the angle of the light."

Meera put her face in her hands.

"So, what do I do?" she said, her voice slightly muffled.

"Nothing yet," Sanya said. "Know it first. Let it be real. Don't perform it."

"And then?"

"And then — at some point — be honest."

Meera looked at her through her fingers.

"Easy for you to say."

Sanya smiled. "Nothing about any of this is easy. I'm just the one who watches from a safe distance."

Rohan passed the amphitheater that Sunday afternoon.

He didn't stop walking. But he slowed, briefly, and glanced at Meera sitting alone on the steps with her notebook.

He kept walking.

He took out his phone and typed a message to no one in his contact list — a draft he saved and never sent, the way he did when he wanted to think out loud without being heard:

She's figuring it out. Good.

He deleted the draft. Put his phone away.

Kept walking.

Chapter 6: Ganesh Festival and The Almost Moment

Pune in Ganesh festival season is not a city that contains a festival.

It is a festival that contains a city.

From the first day of Ganesh Chaturthi, something fundamental shifts in the air. The roads become rivers of colour and sound. Dhol players appear on corners at hours that are nobody's business. The smell of modak and incense and rain-wet marigolds is everywhere. Buildings are draped in lights. Every neighbourhood has its own pandal, its own Bappa, its own particular way of celebrating that has been passed down and argued about and fiercely defended for generations.

And the college campus — which in ordinary times was a fairly self-contained universe — opened its doors and became part of the city's heartbeat.

The cultural committee, which Aarav had supported during his presidency, had organised the college's contribution to the celebrations: a ten-day programme of events culminating in a joint visarjan procession with three neighbouring colleges and the surrounding community.

Geet had volunteered to manage the decoration committee.

This was either a brilliant decision or a catastrophic one, and for the first four days the jury was genuinely out.

Day one of the festival decorations produced the flowers.

Nobody was certain exactly how it happened — Geet's explanation involved a miscommunication with the supplier, a quantity conversion error between dozens and gross, and what she described as "an optimistic interpretation of the budget spreadsheet."

The result was that the college campus woke up on the second morning of Ganesh Chaturthi to discover it had been transformed overnight into something between a botanical garden and a wedding venue.

Marigolds and Hibiscus. Everywhere. Some more colourful flowers that added to the beauty. On the staircases, wound around the corridor railings, cascading from the windows of the admin block, banked in great golden drifts against the library entrance. The amphitheater steps were buried in them. The chai tapri outside the postgrad block had somehow acquired a flower arch.

Geet stood in the middle of the main courtyard at seven-thirty in the morning, surrounded by her decoration committee — five shell-shocked second-year students who had worked through the night — looking at what they had collectively created.

"It's a lot," one of them said.

"It's a lot," Geet agreed.

"The budget—"

"The budget and I have agreed to not discuss each other for a few days."

She was still standing there, working through the logistics in her head, when Venky Sir arrived for his morning walk through the campus. He turned the corner from the staffroom block and stopped.

He looked at the marigolds. He looked at the flower arch over the chai tapri. He looked at the cascade of gold tumbling from the admin block windows.

He looked at Geet.

Geet looked at him with the expression of someone prepared to accept any verdict.

Venky Sir looked back at the marigolds.

"Whoever did this," he said, at normal volume, to no one in particular, "I respect the commitment."

He walked on.

Geet exhaled so deeply that several marigold petals trembled.

The festival days had a quality that the ordinary college year did not.

Something about the dhol in the evenings — audible from the campus, drifting in from the city — and the coloured lights, and the shared sense that the world outside had temporarily suspended its normal rules and replaced them with more interesting ones, made everything feel simultaneously bigger and gentler.

Aarav felt it in the particular way of someone who grew up in Pune and had this festival woven into his earliest memories — the sound of it, the smell of it, the feeling of being part of something old and communal and bigger than yourself.

He said this to Niel one evening, standing at the edge of the campus where you could see the neighbourhood pandal lit up in the middle distance.

"I didn't grow up here," Niel said. "We had the festival in Nashik too. But it felt different."

"How?"

"Smaller. Or maybe I was just watching from further away." He looked at the lights. "Here it feels like it's happening *to* you rather than *near* you."

Aarav nodded. That was exactly it.

"Kabir says you should experience the visarjan procession," Aarav said.

"Kabir says I should experience everything."

"He's not wrong."

Niel looked at the pandal. "I'll go," he said. "To the procession."

"Good."

A pause.

"Aarav." Niel said his name with a particular quality — the way he said most things, directly and without preamble. "The Meera situation."

Aarav went very still.

"I'm not asking," Niel said. "I'm observing. You watch for her reaction before you decide how you feel about things. That's not a friendship habit. That's something else."

The campus went about its evening around them. A drum was practicing somewhere in the distance.

"I know," Aarav said.

"Okay," Niel said.

That was the whole conversation. Niel turned and walked back toward the hostel. Aarav stood at the edge of the campus for another minute, looking at the lights.

You watch for her reaction before you decide how you feel.

He had never put words to it. The words fit perfectly.

The day of the visarjan procession was loud and golden and completely alive.

The college group assembled at the campus gate at five in the evening. All seven of them plus Geet, who had worn a bright yellow kurta and marigold earrings that matched the flowers she had accidentally ordered too many of, which she considered full-circle justice.

The procession came through their neighbourhood at five-thirty — the Bappa from the campus pandal joining the stream of idols from surrounding areas, all moving toward the river. The sound was tremendous. Dhol players, cymbals, firecrackers in careful controlled bursts, the accumulated devotion of ten days finding its release in movement and colour and the particular joyful grief of saying goodbye to something beautiful.

The group moved with the procession. This was the thing about visarjan — you didn't watch it; you were absorbed by it. The crowd moved with its own intelligence, carrying you with it, and within five minutes you had lost your sense of where you were in relation to where you started and it didn't matter at all.

Kabir had immediately found the dhol players and was now contributing enthusiastically to a craft he had no formal training in. A professional dhol player had turned to look at him twice, both times with the expression of a man trying to decide if this was annoying or entertaining.

Geet had found the group of children throwing gulaal powder and was now throwing it back, her yellow kurta acquiring a second colour scheme. She looked genuinely ecstatic.

Sanya was walking steadily through the crowd with the competence of someone who had processed crowds into data — tracking the group's positions, moving efficiently, enjoying herself with a kind of organized thoroughness that was entirely Sanya.

Rohan was in the crowd somewhere. Not far — they could occasionally spot him — but navigating on his own parallel path, the way he always did.

Niel moved through the procession with the calm attentiveness of someone experiencing something for the first time and choosing to experience it completely — not documenting it on his phone, not narrating it, just absorbing it with every sense fully open.

And Aarav and Meera, who had been walking together through the general group, found themselves at some point separated from the others by the natural physics of a crowd in motion — a surge of people moving left, a cluster of children crossing, someone's sound system on a truck cutting between them and the rest — and then they were not with the group anymore.

They were still in the procession. The Bappa was still moving ahead of them. The dhol was still loud and insistent and wonderful.

But it was just them.

They came to the riverbank as the procession reached its destination.

The river at visarjan time is a thing to see. The last light of the September evening coming off the water. Dozens of processions converging from different directions, their lights and sounds meeting and merging. The moment when the idol enters the water — that moment of transformation, of letting go — which is something you cannot fully explain to someone who has not stood there and felt it.

They stood at the edge of the bank.

Around them: the procession, the crowd, the sound, the light. Everywhere was movement and noise and the specific emotion of ten thousand people all feeling something at once.

Between them: quiet.

Not the heavy quiet of something unsaid. The warm quiet of two people who can stand next to each other in the middle of all of this and not need to perform anything.

Aarav looked at the river.

Meera looked at the river.

Then she laughed — softly, to herself — at something, and Aarav turned to look at her.

"What?" he said.

"Nothing. I just—" She shook her head. "I almost didn't come back, you know. To Pune. For postgrad." She looked at him. "And then I think about tonight and I think — what would I have missed?"

Aarav looked at her face in the evening light. The procession colours moving across it. The river behind her.

He opened his mouth.

He did not know exactly what he was going to say. He knew the direction of it — knew it was true and that it had been true for a while and that he was done navigating around it.

From somewhere very close and very loud:

"AARAV. MEERA. THERE YOU ARE. I LOST MY CHAPPAL IN THE CROWD AND SOMEONE HAS TO HELP ME AND—"

Kabir appeared out of the procession with his arms wide, one bare foot held up for evidence, his expression the exact combination of genuine crisis and theatrical presentation that was his specific genius.

The moment dissolved.

Meera laughed — a real one, the kind that comes from below the chest — and turned to help Kabir assess the chappal situation.

Aarav stood there for exactly two more seconds.

He breathed.

He thought: *Soon.*

He turned to help find Kabir's chappal.

They found the rest of the group at the chai tapri near the river an hour later — Sanya at a table with a chai, Geet with gulaal in her hair and an expression of deep satisfaction, Niel quiet and present, Rohan appearing from somewhere with his customary lack of announcement.

Kabir arrived hobbling theatrically, one chappal on, one chappal miraculously recovered from twenty feet upstream.

"The chappal survived," he announced. "As will we all."

Geet started clapping.

"She always claps," Aarav observed.

"I clap for the right things," Geet said with dignity.

They ordered chai. The river was still receiving processions behind them. The city was alive in every direction. The lights were extraordinary.

Niel sat at the edge of the group — not apart from it, just at its edge — and looked at the river for a long moment. Then he said, quietly but clearly enough for everyone to hear:

"I think this is what people mean when they say they miss college. Not the exams. Not even the campus." He paused. "This. Right here."

Nobody responded immediately.

They all just sat with it.

The chai arrived and they drank it while the city put itself to bed around them and the river carried its cargo of let-go things gently downstream into the dark.

Later, on the walk back, Sanya fell into step with Aarav.

"You almost said something tonight," she said.

Not a question.

Aarav said nothing.

"The chappal was bad timing," she said.

"Impeccable timing," Aarav said. "Depending on your perspective."

Sanya looked at him sideways. "Are you scared?"

"Of what?"

"Of being wrong about what she feels."

Aarav walked for a few steps. Honest answer: "Yes."

"That's fair," Sanya said. "But consider the alternative."

She walked ahead to join Geet, who was explaining to Niel in great detail why the gulaal in her hair was actually an improvement.

Aarav walked alone for a moment in the middle of the group.

Somewhere up ahead, Meera was laughing at something Kabir had said.

She turned her head — not toward Kabir, but back, instinctively, the way you turn when you want to share something good with a specific person.

She turned toward Aarav.

He caught her eye.

She smiled.

He smiled back.

It lasted about one second.

It was enough.

Chapter 7: Kabir's Serious Moment

There were signs, if you knew where to look.

The first sign was that Kabir missed a morning chai.

This sounds small. It was not small. Kabir had not missed a morning chai in three years of college. He treated the ten-thirty tapri run with the religious consistency of someone who had made a personal covenant with the universe and intended to honour it.

The second sign was that he was quiet at lunch.

Not performatively quiet. Not the quiet of someone saving energy for a bigger punchline. Just — absent. Present in body, elsewhere in mind. He ate his food, looked at his plate, contributed nothing to the conversation except occasional nods that were slightly delayed, like a signal reaching him from a distance.

Sanya noticed on day one.

Meera noticed on day two.

Aarav noticed on day two also, but said nothing, which was its own kind of noticing.

By day three, even Geet — who had the observational focus of someone in the middle of their own continuous film — paused mid-sentence during lunch, looked at Kabir, and said: "You're not being funny."

"I'm always funny," Kabir said.

"You said that without any energy. That's not funny. That's just a sentence."

Kabir looked. Said nothing.

Geet looked at Aarav. Aarav gave her the smallest headshake. *Not now.*

Geet, to her credit, understood immediately and went back to her food.

He also missed an internal assessment.

This was the thing that confirmed it was serious, because Kabir's relationship with academic deadlines was one of his few genuinely disciplined qualities. He was not a studious person in the conventional sense — he did not make colour-coded notes or revise three weeks in advance — but he showed up. Always. For exams, for presentations, for assessments that counted.

He missed this one.

Dr. Desai noted the absence without comment in class. Aarav sent Kabir a message. The reply came forty minutes later:

I'll sort it.

Three words. No punctuation theatrics. No joke at the end.

Aarav stared at his phone.

Then he put it in his pocket, finished his lecture, and went to find Kabir.

He found him on the hostel terrace at seven in the evening.

Kabir was sitting on the water tank ledge — a spot they had used in first year for conversations they didn't want the rest of the world to hear — looking at the Pune skyline doing its dusk thing. The city was beginning to light up. The Western Ghats were a dark outline against the orange sky.

Aarav sat next to him.

He did not say anything.

This was important. The wrong opening would close everything. Kabir was the kind of person who could deflect any question with a joke if he saw the question coming — it was both his gift and his armour. The only way through was to not make it a question. Just sit. Let the silence do its work.

It took eleven minutes.

Then Kabir said: "My dad called on Sunday."

"Okay."

"He wants me to join the business after graduation." A pause. "Not wants. Expects."

Aarav said nothing. Let it continue.

"We have a wholesale textile business in Ulhasnagar. My grandfather started it; my dad grew it. It's a real business.

Good money. My dad's not a bad person." Kabir turned the chai cup in his hands — a cup he'd brought up and hadn't drunk from. "He's a good person, actually. He just — he has a plan. For me. He's had it since I was twelve years old and I don't think it occurred to him that I might have a different one."

"What's your plan?" Aarav asked.

Kabir was quiet for a moment.

"Media," he said finally. The word came out like something he had been carrying in a closed fist for a long time. "Content. Storytelling. I don't know exactly what shape yet — writing, video, something. I just know that every time I make someone laugh, or I tell a story and I can feel the room change — " He stopped. "That's the only time I feel like I'm doing something I was supposed to do."

The skyline went about its business. A train horn somewhere in the distance.

"I've never said that out loud," Kabir said. "To anyone."

"I know," Aarav said.

"How do you know?"

"Because you've been carrying it alone. I can tell." Aarav looked at him. "How long?"

"Since second year probably. When I started that college meme page."

"That page had twelve thousand followers."

"I know." Something flickered in Kabir's expression — the ghost of the usual grin, real underneath all the weight. "My dad thinks I was wasting time."

Aarav sat with that.

"I make everyone laugh," Kabir said, quieter now, "because if I stop — I have to think about what I actually want. And then I have to figure out how to want it out loud, in front of my family, and that's — " He exhaled. "That's scarier than anything this campus has ever thrown at me."

Aarav did not give advice.

He did not say *talk to your dad* or *follow your dreams* or any of the other things that are true in theory and useless at the specific weight of a specific Tuesday evening.

He said: "Then let's figure it out. Together. Properly."

Kabir looked at him.

"You don't have to solve it alone," Aarav said. "You never had to."

Kabir looked back at the city.

He didn't say anything for a while.

Then he drank his chai — cold by now, completely undrinkable — and made a face.

"This is terrible."

"You've had it sitting there for half an hour."

"Cold chai is an act of violence."

"Then why did you drink it?"

"Because the moment felt right and I didn't want to ruin it by getting up." He looked at Aarav. "Can we get a fresh one?"

Aarav stood up.

"Obviously," he said.

He fell asleep that night with his phone on his chest. The competition submission portal still open on the screen. The green confirmation tick glowing quietly in the dark.

Done, he had thought, before sleep took him. *Whatever happens now.*

He did not know that three floors below, in the media lab, something was already happening.

Venky Sir called Kabir to his office the next morning.

He did not mention the missed assessment. He did not mention the three quiet days, or the cold chai on the terrace, or any of it. He simply poured two cups — one for himself, one that he placed on the corner of the desk in Kabir's direction without announcement — and said:

"Tell me something, Kabir. If failure was not possible — what would you do?"

Kabir opened his mouth to make a joke.

Stopped.

The question was too clean for a joke. It had no edges to deflect off.

He thought about it honestly, which was what the question was designed to produce.

"Media," he said. "Storytelling. Something where I get to make people feel things on purpose."

Venky Sir nodded slowly. As if this was not a surprise. As if this was, in fact, exactly what he had expected to hear and had been waiting for Kabir to say.

"Then you already know what you want," he said. He picked up his chai. "The rest is just courage." A pause. The particular Venky Sir pause that meant the next sentence was the one that mattered. "And courage, Kabir, is not the absence of fear. It is the decision that something else is more important than the fear."

Kabir sat with that.

"What if my dad doesn't understand?"

"He might not. Not immediately." Venky Sir looked at him with that steady, seen-everything gaze. "But parents who love their children — and yours does — eventually want the right thing more than they want their own plan. Give him time. But first give him the truth."

Kabir nodded slowly.

He picked up the extra chai cup from the corner of the desk. Drank it.

"Sir," he said.

"Hmm."

"How do you always know?"

Venky Sir smiled — the real one, the one that reached his eyes. "I've had this conversation many times, Kabir. With different names in the chair. The specifics change. The fear doesn't."

He turned back to his desk.

"Go to class," he said.

Kabir went.

Meera heard part of it.

Not the terrace conversation — that was private, and Aarav kept it. But she was in the hostel common room when Kabir came back from Venky Sir's office, and she saw his face.

She had known Kabir for three years. She knew every variation of his expression — the performative ones, the real ones, the ones in between. What she saw on his face now she had never seen before.

Relief. The specific relief of someone who has put down something heavy and is still slightly amazed by how light their arms feel.

She watched him cross the common room. He spotted her. For a moment he just looked at her — clearly, without deflection.

"You, okay?" she said.

"Getting there," he said. "Yeah."

He walked on.

She sat with what she had seen.

Here is what became clear to Meera in that moment, quietly and without drama:

She loved Kabir. She would always love Kabir. The way you love someone who has been your safe place in a difficult year — fully, permanently, without condition.

But it was not the love she had confused it for.

It had never been that. She had borrowed a label from the wrong shelf and put it on something that already had its own name.

She opened her notebook that evening.

She did not write anything new.

She crossed out nothing.

She simply sat with the clarity of something finally correctly named, and it felt like putting a room back in order after a long time of not quite being able to find anything.

Chapter 7B: The Entry

The Resonance Creative Award had been announced in the second week of the semester.

It was on the notice board for three days before Kabir stopped at it — which was two days and twenty-three hours longer than it took everyone else to walk past it. He read it once. Then again. Cash prize. Recommendation letter to a partnered media production company in Mumbai. External judges from outside the college. Submissions open to all postgrad students.

He took a photograph of the notice on his phone. Did not mention it to anyone.

The competition was the first serious thing he had wanted in a long time. Which meant it was also the first serious thing he was afraid of. These two conditions, he was learning, almost always arrived together.

He had noticed Vikram Nair without particularly meaning to.

Third week of semester. Media lab. Kabir had gone in to book equipment — the college had two decent cameras available for student use, sign-up sheet on the door — and there was a senior student already at the desk. Tall. Good watch. The specific ease of someone who had never once worried about whether the room would accommodate him.

He signed out both cameras for the following weekend.

Kabir looked at the sheet after he left. Both cameras. The whole weekend.

He booked his slot for the weekday instead. Told himself it didn't matter.

It didn't matter. Until it did.

Kabir sat alone in the media lab at eleven-fifteen at night.

This was unusual for two reasons. First, Kabir avoided being alone the way most people avoided root canals — instinctively, consistently, with a vague sense that nothing good came from it. Second, Kabir was never in any lab at eleven-fifteen at night. He believed strongly that nothing academic was worth doing after ten and had maintained this position through three years of evidence.

But this was not academic.

This was his.

The project had taken six weeks.

He had not told anyone the full shape of it — not Aarav, not Meera, not even Sanya who knew most things about most people before they knew themselves. He had mentioned it in passing. *Something I'm working on.* The way you mention something you are afraid to jinx by describing too specifically.

It was a short documentary. Twenty-two minutes. About the campus — but not the campus of brochures and orientation presentations. The real one. The chai tapri at seven in the morning when the first students arrived still half-asleep. The library at midnight during exam season — the particular quality of that silence, forty people breathing the same tired air. The notice board and the hands that stopped at it. The amphitheater in the rain.

He had filmed it on his phone and a borrowed camera. He had edited it across fourteen late nights. He had added no narration — just the sounds of the place itself, and occasionally, briefly, students talking. Not performing for the camera. Just being.

It was the most honest thing he had ever made.

He watched it one final time on the lab monitor.

Twenty-two minutes.

He did not make a single adjustment.

Then he opened the competition submission portal — the annual Resonance Creative Award, external judges, cash prize, and a recommendation letter to a partnered media company that he had read about four times and pretended he hadn't.

He filled in the form.

He attached the file.

He sat with the mouse over the submit button for a moment that was longer than a moment.

He thought about his father. About the phone call that hadn't happened yet but needed to. About one year of trust and what it would mean to have something real to show for the first month of it.

He thought about Venky Sir's question.

If failure was not possible — what would you do?

He clicked submit.

The portal confirmed receipt. A small green tick. Completely anticlimactic. The most important thing he had done in twenty-two years and the universe responded with a green tick and a reference number.

He leaned back in his chair.

Looked at the ceiling.

Said quietly to nobody:

"Okay. It's out there now."

He did not notice the person at the computer three stations away.

He had not noticed him come in — Kabir had been too deep inside the edit to notice much of anything for the last two hours. He did not notice him now because he was already packing his bag, already thinking about sleep, already carrying the particular lightness of someone who has finally done the thing they were afraid to do.

He did not notice the nice watch.

He did not notice the way the person waited — completely still — until Kabir had left the lab.

He did not notice the screen that came to life three stations away, navigating quietly to the competition submission portal.

The lab was empty now.

The campus was quiet.

The green tick glowed on a monitor that nobody was watching anymore.

Outside, walking back to the hostel, Kabir looked at the sky.

Pune at midnight had its own particular beauty — the city never fully slept, always one layer of sound underneath the quiet, always a light somewhere that had no business being on at this hour.

He pulled out his phone.

He almost called his father.

He decided against it. Not yet. Wait for the result. Give him something concrete. Give him the proof that this is real and not just his son's comfortable dream.

He put his phone away.

He walked back to the hostel with the step of someone who has posted the letter and now must simply wait for the reply.

He did not know that the letter had already been opened.

He did not know that someone else was already writing a reply in his name.

He went to sleep.

He slept well, which was the last night for a while that he would.

Chapter 8: Rohan's Grey Move

It started with a notice.

Third week of October, a printed sheet appeared on the postgrad department board — the physical one, the kind people still read because it was positioned next to the water cooler and boredom did the rest. The notice was from the internal assessment committee, signed by Dr. Kulkarni, announcing revised marking criteria for the semester's continuous assessment component.

The revision was, in plain terms, unfair.

It restructured the weightage in a way that disproportionately penalised students who had performed well on practical and participation — which was most of the postgrad batch — in favour of written theory marks, which happened to suit a much smaller group. The language was technical enough to confuse on first reading. The implication, when you worked through it, was clear.

By evening, the postgrad batch's group chat had forty-seven messages about it.

By the next morning, a second-year student named Priya Joshi — quiet, thorough, the kind of person who read the fine print on everything — had done the full calculation and posted a detailed breakdown showing exactly how the revision affected individual grade trajectories.

The chat went from forty-seven messages to two hundred and twelve.

That afternoon, Rohan went to the administration office.

The group found out because Sanya saw him going in, which she mentioned to Aarav casually, which became a conversation, which became a problem when, two hours later, news filtered back that Rohan had gone in apparently to *support* the committee's decision.

The message arrived in fragments, the way college news always does — incomplete, imprecise, shaped by the telling.

Kabir put it simply: "Rohan went to bat for the administration?"

"That's what Priya said," Sanya said. "Her friend was in the corridor outside the office."

Aarav's jaw tightened. The particular tightening that came with a specific kind of disappointment — the kind you feel toward someone you had just about started trusting again.

"Why?" Meera said.

Nobody had an answer.

Niel, who had been listening from the edge of the conversation, said: "Wait."

Everyone looked at him.

"Before we react," he said — and there was no judgment in his voice, just the flat practicality of someone who had learned to pause before concluding — "why would Rohan do this? What does he gain?"

Silence.

Kabir opened his mouth. Closed it.

"The administration doesn't owe him anything," Niel continued. "He's a student. He's affected by this revision the same as everyone else. So, what's the logic?"

"Maybe there's no logic," Kabir said. "Maybe he's just—"

"There's always logic," Niel said. "You just haven't found it yet."

Aarav looked at him. Something shifted — the beginning of a different way of reading the situation.

"So, we wait?" Sanya said.

"We watch," Niel said.

They watched.

The next forty-eight hours were interesting.

Rohan continued to appear aligned with the administration's position. He attended the student-faculty meeting on the subject and sat on the committee side of the room, which caused visible ripples. He said very little but what he said seemed measured — slightly ambiguous, tipped just enough to appear sympathetic to the administration without being fully declarative about it.

Priya Joshi, meanwhile, had been building her case. She was meticulous and calm and clearly intended to file a formal complaint through the university grievance channel — which was the correct path but the slow one, the kind that took weeks and generated paperwork and often dissipated in the system before reaching any resolution.

On the third day, Rohan came to the amphitheater.

He sat at his usual end. Said nothing for a few minutes.

Then he said, without looking up from his phone: "Priya needs the internal committee correspondence. The emails between Kulkarni and the assessment office. The revision was requested by a third party — not by the committee itself. She needs that thread."

Quiet.

"How would she get that?" Aarav said carefully.

"She would need someone on the inside who had been trusted enough to be given access to the shared committee folder." A pause. "Someone who appeared to be supporting their position."

The amphitheater processed this.

"You were getting information," Sanya said.

Rohan said nothing.

"That's why you went in. That's why you sat on their side of the room." Sanya stared at him. "You were building access."

Rohan looked up finally. His expression was unreadable — the standard Rohan expression, the one that gave nothing away and never had.

"The emails are on a shared drive," he said. "The folder link is accessible if you know the path. Priya's complaint needs evidence that the revision was externally pressured, not internally generated. Without that, it's just students disagreeing with professors, which goes nowhere."

He looked at Aarav.

"She files it with the right evidence, the revision gets reviewed, probably reversed. Without it, Kulkarni buries it."

Silence.

Kabir said: "You spent three days being the bad guy so you could get the folder link."

Rohan said nothing. Which was, with Rohan, an answer.

"Why didn't you just tell us?" Meera asked.

The question sat there.

Rohan looked at her steadily. "Because if I'd told you, you'd have told Priya, Priya would have changed her behaviour, and Kulkarni would have known the strategy. The only way it worked was if my support looked genuine."

"You let us think—"

"Yes," Rohan said simply.

Aarav sat with this.

"That's exhausting," he said finally. "Living like that."

"Sometimes," Rohan said.

He stood up. Sent something from his phone — presumably the folder path to someone, presumably Priya. Then he put his phone away.

"Rohan," Aarav said.

He stopped.

"Why don't you ever just tell people what you're doing?"

Rohan looked at him. Something moved in his expression — small, deep, honest for exactly a moment.

"Because then it stops working," he said.

He walked away.

The campus gate was nearly empty by then.

Rohan stood near the closed chai stall outside the wall; phone pressed against his ear.

"Yeah," he said quietly.

Pause.

"I handled it."

Another pause.

His expression hardened slightly.

"No," he said finally. "They still don't know."

The call ended.

For a few seconds, he stayed there looking back toward the academic block — toward the lights still glowing in second-floor classrooms.

Then he put the phone away and walked into the Pune night without looking back.

Niel and Venky Sir had chai that evening.

Their by-now-established ritual: the corridor window, the second chai cup that appeared without ceremony, conversation that wandered wherever it needed to go.

Niel told him about Rohan.

Venky Sir listened without interrupting — a skill, Niel had realised, that was rarer than it looked. Most people listened in order to respond. Venky Sir listened in order to understand, which was an entirely different activity.

When Niel finished, Venky Sir was quiet for a moment.

"Two kinds of misunderstood people," he said finally. He turned his cup slowly in his hands — that gesture that meant he was selecting his words with care. "Some are misunderstood because they are genuinely difficult to understand. Unclear. Inconsistent. They create the confusion themselves." He looked at the campus below. "And some are misunderstood because the world is not patient enough to understand them. They are clear — but their clarity operates on a frequency that requires effort to tune into."

He looked at Niel.

"Which kind is Rohan?"

Niel thought about it honestly. "The second."

Venky Sir nodded slowly.

"Then the question," he said, "is not what Rohan is doing. The question is what he is protecting." He picked up his chai. "That answer — I suspect — will take a while longer to find."

He sipped.

Outside, the campus evening settled around them, unhurried and ordinary and full of things quietly becoming what they would eventually be.

Priya filed the complaint four days later.

With the correspondence as evidence — and Niel's quietly precise guidance on how to structure the grievance to match the university's formal review criteria — the complaint reached the Dean's office as a complete, documented, procedurally correct case rather than an emotional student objection.

The Dean ordered a review.

Two weeks later, the marking revision was reversed.

Dr. Kulkarni said nothing to the postgrad batch directly. But he stopped using yellowed pages and started answering questions from the second row.

Priya sent a message to the batch group: *Revision reversed. Thank you all.* She did not know who specifically to thank, because nobody had told her. Nobody told her.

Rohan saw the message. Put his phone away. Went back to whatever he had been reading.

Aarav watched him from across the library.

He thought about what Venky Sir had apparently said — second kind, not first kind. He thought about Rohan's specific brand of grey — always there, always operating, always at a slight angle to visible.

What is he protecting?

He didn't know yet.

But he was starting to ask the right question.

Chapter 9: What Aarav Finally Admits

The problem with knowing something is that once you know it, you cannot unknow it.

Aarav had been trying anyway.

He had been trying for approximately six weeks — which was, if he was being honest with himself, not trying at all but simply the act of giving something a different name and hoping the name would change the thing. He had called it *closeness.* He had called it *familiarity.* He had called it *the natural result of working on a project together in a library at eleven at night.*

None of these names fit. He knew they didn't fit. He kept using them anyway because the correct name required doing something about it, and doing something about it required a courage that kept arriving at the door and then quietly leaving without knocking.

He noticed everything now. That was the problem with knowing.

He noticed the specific way she tucked her pen behind her ear when she was thinking. He noticed that she laughed at Kabir's jokes a half-second after everyone else — not because she was slow, but because she was actually listening rather than anticipating. He noticed that when she was tired, she got quieter, and when she was happy, she got louder in a way she seemed unaware of. He noticed these things the way you notice things you have no business noticing this precisely.

He was, in short, a complete disaster.

It was Niel who finally said it plainly.

They were on the terrace of the hostel on a Wednesday evening — just the two of them, which happened sometimes now, the easy way it happens between people who have found each other's company uncomplicated. Niel had a book. Aarav had his phone, which he had been staring at without reading for eleven minutes.

Niel turned a page.

"You're not looking at your phone," he said. "You're looking through it."

"I'm reading."

"You haven't scrolled in eleven minutes."

Aarav put the phone down.

Niel read another paragraph. Closed his book on his finger. Looked at Aarav with that direct, unhurried attention.

"Tell me," he said.

Aarav looked at the city.

He had not planned to tell anyone. He had specifically planned to not tell anyone until he had figured out what to do with it, which at the current rate of progress meant approximately never.

But there was something about the way Niel asked — without curiosity, without the slight hungry lean that most people brought to other people's problems — that made it feel safe to say the true thing.

So, Aarav said it.

Not dramatically. Not with the full architecture of every feeling, he had been constructing for six weeks. Just the plain version.

"I'm in love with Meera."

The city hummed. A dog barked twice somewhere below.

"I know," Niel said.

Aarav turned to look at him. "You know?"

"Everyone knows. Except possibly Meera, but I suspect she also knows." He reopened his book. "What are you afraid of?"

"That she doesn't feel the same."

"What else?"

Aarav thought about it honestly. "That she does feel the same and I still somehow manage to ruin it."

Niel nodded slowly. Not dismissively — with the specific nod of someone who considers this a legitimate concern and is respecting it.

"Both fears are reasonable," he said. "Neither one is a reason to do nothing."

"Easy to say."

"Yes," Niel agreed simply. He did not argue with this. "You came to ask me what to do. But you already know what to do. You're just hoping someone will tell you a way that skips the scared part."

Aarav said nothing.

"There isn't one," Niel said.

He went back to his book.

They sat in comfortable silence for a while. The city below them had no opinion on the matter and went about its evening without comment.

Then Aarav said: "How do you do that?"

"Do what?"

"Say exactly the right thing without making it feel like advice."

Niel thought about it. "Because I'm not trying to fix it," he said. "I just — say what I see."

Aarav looked at him for a moment.

"Venky Sir does the same thing," he said.

Something quiet moved across Niel's expression. "I know," he said. "I noticed that too."

Meera, meanwhile, had arrived at her own crisis point by a different road.

The notebook had been open on her desk for three days. The word was still there in the margin — small, certain, written weeks ago. She had not added to it. She had not needed to. It was enough.

The problem was not knowing. The problem was that knowing without acting had a shelf life, and she was approaching the end of it.

She went to Sanya.

She knocked on Sanya's door at nine in the evening, which was late enough to signal seriousness and early enough to not be an emergency. Sanya opened the door, looked at Meera's face, and stepped back wordlessly to let her in.

They sat on the floor — Sanya's room was the kind where floor-sitting happened naturally, books everywhere, a string of lights along one wall.

"I have to do something about it," Meera said.

"Yes," Sanya said.

"I've been sitting with it for weeks."

"I know."

"If I say something and he doesn't—" She stopped. Started again. "The friendship. I don't want to—"

"Meera." Sanya said her name with a gentleness that also contained finality. "The friendship is already different. It's been different for a while. You both know it. Pretending it isn't is not protecting it."

Meera looked at the string lights.

"What if it goes wrong?"

"Things can go wrong either way," Sanya said. "At least one of those ways involves you being honest."

A pause.

"When did you get this wise?" Meera asked.

"I've always been this wise," Sanya said. "You were just too busy being confused to notice."

Meera laughed — the real kind. The tension broke slightly.

"Okay," she said.

"Okay," Sanya said.

"I'm going to — I'm going to say something. Soon."

"Soon is not a date."

"This week."

"Better," Sanya said. She handed Meera a biscuit from the packet on her desk. "Now tell me you haven't eaten dinner."

"I haven't eaten dinner."

Sanya stood up with the efficiency of someone for whom feeding her friends was a moral obligation. "Come on. Canteen."

It happened on a Thursday evening.

Not because Thursday was chosen. Not because the circumstances had been arranged. It happened the way real things tend to happen — because all the preconditions had been quietly building for months and the moment simply arrived when both people were finally willing to be in it.

The campus was quiet. Exam revision season had unofficially begun — the library was full; the corridors were less so. The amphitheater in the evening had become the territory of people who needed air and silence in equal measure.

Aarav was there first. He had been trying to read. He had been failing to read. He was watching the Pune skyline do its dusk-to-dark transition, which it did with particular beauty that time of year.

Meera arrived ten minutes later.

She saw him. She sat down. Not at a distance — beside him, the way she always did, close enough that their arms were almost touching. The way that had been normal between them for years and had recently become something he was acutely, precisely aware of.

"Revision?" she said.

"Attempting," he said.

She put her own book on the step beside her without opening it. They both sat looking at the skyline.

Something had shifted in the air between them. Something different from the usual warmth — more charged, slightly breathless, the feeling of standing at the edge of something and knowing the step is coming.

Both of them felt it.

Neither of them spoke for a full two minutes.

Then Aarav turned toward her.

He had not prepared a speech. He had specifically decided not to prepare a speech because speeches gave you something to hide behind, and he was done hiding behind things.

"Meera," he said.

She turned to look at him.

Their eyes met — really met, the kind of meeting that doesn't look away after the polite one second.

"I need to say something," he said. "And I want to say it properly, not sideways or by accident or in the middle of something else." He took a breath. "I've been in love with you for a while now. I don't know the exact day it started, which probably means it didn't start on a day — it just became obvious slowly and then all at once." He paused. "I kept waiting for the perfect moment but I think the perfect moment is just any moment where I'm being completely honest. So, that's what this is."

Silence.

The kind that is not empty.

Meera looked at him.

Her expression moved through several things very quickly — something that looked like relief, something that looked like the specific emotion of hearing a thing you've been hoping for and not quite believing you're hearing it.

Then she said:

"Took you long enough."

He laughed. He couldn't help it — the laugh came out of somewhere below all the nervousness, the genuine released kind.

"Yeah?" he said.

"Yes." she said. "A while. For me too." She looked at him steadily. "The dupatta."

"What?"

"The night you fell asleep at the library table. I put my dupatta on your shoulders and sat there and I thought —" She shook her head slightly, smiling. "I thought, *oh.* Just like that. *Oh.*"

He looked at her.

"That was six weeks ago," he said.

"I know."

"You've known for six weeks."

"I needed to be sure."

"And?"

She held his gaze. Clear. Certain. No performance.

"Sure," she said.

The amphitheater was quiet around them. The city glowed in the middle distance. Somewhere behind them the campus went on being the campus.

And between them — after months of almost-moments and wrong timing and chappal-related interruptions and the specific beautiful frustration of two people circling the same true thing — something settled. Warmly. Completely.

Not with a grand gesture. Not with a filmy moment. Just with two people sitting close in the evening light, finally saying the honest thing, and the world not ending. In fact, the world being, if anything, slightly more itself than it had been before.

Kabir saw it from the corridor above.

He had come up for air from the library — revision headache, needed five minutes — and he had the perfect elevated view of the amphitheater below.

He watched.

He saw Aarav turn. He saw the conversation he couldn't hear. He saw Meera's expression move through those several things. He saw them both laugh.

He pumped his fist once, silently, with great feeling.

Then he pulled out his phone and opened the group chat.

He typed: IT HAPPENED.

Then deleted it.

He put his phone away.

Some things you celebrate quietly. Inside. Just for yourself, because you have been watching two good people find their way to each other for months and you are genuinely, completely happy about it.

He stood at the corridor railing for another moment.

He smiled to himself.

Then he went back to the library.

Venky Sir found out the way Venky Sir always found out things — not because anyone told him, but because he paid attention to the world in finer grain than most people did.

He noticed it the next morning. The way Aarav and Meera walked into class with the same unhurried timing. The way Meera passed him chai first without thinking. The way Aarav said something quiet and Meera smiled before the sentence was finished.

That afternoon he called Aarav to his office.

He did not mention any of it directly. He asked about the semester project. He gave feedback on the research methodology section. He refilled his chai.

Then he said, apparently to the window:

"The best relationships are built on the same foundation as the best friendships. Honesty. Patience. The ability to sit in silence without discomfort."

Aarav said nothing.

Venky Sir slid the second chai cup across the desk.

"Don't overthink it," he said. "Just be good to each other."

He turned back to his papers.

Aarav picked up the chai cup. Drank it.

He looked at the photograph on Venky Sir's desk — a small one, in the corner, partially obscured by a stack of files. A woman's face. A smile that was not performative. Eyes that were intelligent and warm and completely at ease.

He had noticed the photograph before. He had never asked.

He didn't ask now either.

He just sat for a moment in the quiet of the office, drinking his chai, while Venky Sir worked and the campus went about its afternoon.

Then he left.

Venky Sir looked at the photograph.

He took a long, slow sip.

Said nothing.

Chapter 10: Sanya Finds Herself

It began with a question.

The most important things often do. Not the large dramatic questions — *What is the meaning of life, what is my purpose, where am I going* — but the small honest ones. The kind you can only ask yourself on an ordinary afternoon when nobody is watching and you have accidentally run out of things to keep yourself busy with.

Sanya ran out of things on a Saturday.

This was unusual. Sanya was not a person who ran out of things. She had a semester plan, a reading list, a personal development goal sheet that was reviewed and updated monthly. She was constitutionally opposed to unstructured time. She had once described a free afternoon as "an administrative failure."

But on this particular Saturday the plan was complete, the reading was done, the notes were organised, and the library closed early.

She sat at her desk.

She looked at her colour-coded notebook.

And she thought — clearly, for possibly the first time in a long time — *what do I actually want to do right now?*

Not what should be done. Not what was productive. Not what moved her forward toward any particular goal.

What did she *want?*

She sat with the question for a long moment.

It was a stranger than expected feeling. Like opening a door in a familiar house and finding a room you hadn't known was there.

Geet knocked at four o'clock.

She arrived with two cutting chais from the tapri — holding them with the careful focus of someone transporting something important — and an expression that suggested she had somewhere to be but had decided Sanya was more important.

She handed Sanya a chai. Sat on the floor cross-legged without being invited, which was simply how Geet operated and which Sanya had stopped finding strange two weeks in.

"You look like you're solving a maths problem that doesn't have numbers," Geet said.

"I was thinking."

"About what?"

Sanya looked at her chai. "What makes me happy."

Geet considered this with the full seriousness she brought to genuinely interesting questions. "And?"

"I'm not sure I've asked myself that directly before."

Geet stared. "Never?"

"Not — not like this." Sanya set the chai down. "I've always asked *what should I do* or *what makes sense* or *what is the correct next step.* But just — what makes me happy?" She paused. "It felt like an indulgent question."

Geet looked at her for a long moment.

"Sanya," she said. "That is possibly the saddest thing I have ever heard."

"It's not sad. It's practical."

"It's both." Geet wrapped her hands around her chai cup. "Okay. So, what makes you happy? Actually happy, not productive happy."

Sanya opened her mouth. Closed it.

She thought about it with the same honesty she brought to every serious thing.

She thought about the morning library sessions when she had a whole table to herself and three hours without interruption. She thought about the FC Road evenings with the group — the specific warmth of that, the easy loud laughter of people who knew each other. She thought about the satisfaction of a well-argued point landing in class. She thought about Geet appearing at her door with chai. She thought about Meera resting her head on her shoulder during a Kabir punchline.

She thought about Pune in the morning, the city waking up in stages. She thought about the particular pleasure of a good paragraph in a good book. She thought about being trusted with a secret, being the person someone came to.

She listed these things.

All of them involved her own mind, her friendships, her city, her own quiet world.

None of them involved a romantic love story.

She sat with this.

"I think," she said slowly, "that I've been treating my life like a problem to solve."

Geet was very still.

"Like there's a correct sequence — study, career, relationship, stability — and I've been working through the sequence without asking whether the sequence was mine." She looked at the string lights. "I've been waiting for something. But I don't think I've ever clearly decided what."

"Maybe it's not a thing to wait for," Geet said quietly. "Maybe it's just — a story to live."

Sanya looked at her.

Geet was sometimes, underneath the chaos and the wrong classrooms and the accidental chai disasters, entirely, simply wise. She did not know she was being wise, which was perhaps why it landed so cleanly.

"Yes," Sanya said.

They sat with that for a while.

Two days later, Sanya went to Venky Sir.

Not with a question exactly. More with the need to say something out loud to someone who would hear it properly.

She sat in the chair across from his desk and said: "I think I've been measuring myself against a version of life that isn't mine."

Venky Sir looked at her over his chai cup. He did not respond immediately — he let the sentence sit, gave it the respect of full consideration.

"Tell me more," he said.

"Everyone around me has something," she said. "Aarav has his leadership, his purpose. Meera has her clarity. Kabir has his dreams even when they scare him. And I have — plans. I have very good plans." She looked at her hands. "But I've been confusing planning with living. And I've been confusing not being in a romantic relationship with something being wrong with me."

Silence.

"Is something wrong with you?" Venky Sir asked.

"No," she said. Clearly. Without hesitation.

"Good," he said. "Because there isn't." He set his cup down. "Sanya, the world is very loud about what a life should contain and in what order. Relationship, family, the complete set." He looked at her steadily. "But there is no universal sequence. There is only your sequence. And your sequence—" he gestured at her, at the whole organised, sharp, quietly extraordinary person of her "—appears to be running very well."

She looked at him.

"Not everyone's journey has a romantic chapter," he said. "Some of the greatest love stories are between a person and their own life." A pause. "And some begin later, and some begin differently, and some are still being written in ways you can't see from here."

"What if mine doesn't have one?"

"Then it has other things," he said simply. "And those things are not consolation prizes. They are the actual prizes." He picked up his chai. "Stop apologising for the shape of your life, Sanya. It is a very good shape."

She sat with that.

Then she said: "You always know exactly what to say."

Venky Sir made a sound that was almost a laugh. "I have had many conversations in this chair. I have made many mistakes outside it. The knowing comes from the mistakes, not from the wisdom." He looked at her. "Remember that. Knowledge without experience is just vocabulary."

The conversation with Meera happened that evening.

They were in Sanya's room — Meera had come to tell her about Aarav, which she did with the specific brightness of someone who has resolved a long tension and is still slightly amazed by the lightness of it.

Sanya listened to the whole thing. She smiled at the right moments. She asked the right questions.

Then Meera looked at her and said: "You knew."

"For a while."

"And you didn't say anything."

"It wasn't mine to say." Sanya looked at her. "You needed to find it yourself."

Meera shook her head slowly. "Three years," she said. "We've been in each other's lives for three years and I still feel like I'm only just seeing how much you pay attention."

"I pay attention to the things that matter," Sanya said.

Meera moved across the room and hugged her — the full, genuine kind, not the side-hug of casual greeting.

Sanya held it.

Then Meera pulled back and looked at her properly. The way Meera looked at things when she was being fully present.

"Are you happy?" she asked. Just like that. Simple and direct.

Sanya thought about the question she had asked herself on Saturday. About the list. About Geet and chai and morning libraries and this room and this person asking her this exact question.

"Yes," she said. "I actually think I am."

Meera smiled. "Good."

"Surprisingly so," Sanya said.

They sat together for a while after that — not talking about anything in particular, just being in the same room in the easy way of two people who had known each other long enough to not need a reason for it.

Outside, the campus settled into its evening rhythms. Somewhere in the city a dhol was practicing, faint and celebratory. The Pune night smelled of old rain and the general busy warmth of a city that never quite goes fully quiet.

Inside, nothing dramatic was happening.

Just two people, sitting together, both of them quietly, completely themselves.

Which is, when you think about it, one of the rarest and most valuable things there is.

Chapter 10B: The Fight

For two weeks after submitting his project Kabir had been quietly, privately hopeful.

Not loudly. Not in the Kabir way of making everything a performance. This was the other Kabir — the one who existed underneath the punchlines, who felt things in the serious way that serious things deserved. He checked the competition portal three times a day. He told nobody. He made jokes about everything else. He slept adequately. He called his father once and spoke about ordinary things and did not mention the documentary or the competition or the recommendation letter that would mean everything if it arrived.

He was waiting the way people wait when they have put something real into the world and must now simply trust it.

He had been so careful. Or so he had thought.

What he did not know — what none of them knew yet — was that Rohan had seen Vikram coming out of the media lab at midnight. Three weeks ago. The night after Kabir had submitted.

Rohan had been walking back from the administrative block — his usual late-night route, the one nobody questioned because Rohan was simply always somewhere nobody expected. He had seen Vikram. Had noted the time. Had noted the expression — the specific settled look of someone who has completed a task they are satisfied with.

Rohan had filed it.

He had been filing things about Vikram for a year. Waiting for the moment when the file was full enough to mean something. Waiting for the right people to be around him when he opened it.

He had not expected it to be Kabir.

That was the one thing he had gotten wrong. And it sat in him heavily — the specific weight of a preparation that was correct in every way except the one that mattered most.

The notice went up on a Tuesday.

Small. Printed. Pinned to the postgrad department board next to the water cooler where everyone stopped and nobody admitted to reading.

RESONANCE CREATIVE AWARD — RESULT DECLARATION

First Prize — Vikram Nair. *Campus Unseen.* A short documentary on college life.

Kabir read it at eight-fifteen in the morning.

He read it twice.

Then he stood very still for a moment in the way of someone whose internal architecture has just shifted and who needs a second to locate the floor again.

Then he walked to class.

He did not tell anyone for two hours.

Aarav noticed at ten-thirty.

Not because Kabir said anything. Because Kabir said nothing — which was the loudest possible communication from a person whose baseline was constant sound. He sat through the entire lecture without a single comment, without a whispered joke, without the small running commentary he provided on everything as a matter of personal principle.

He was completely flat.

Aarav had known Kabir for three years. He had seen him tired, seen him stressed, seen him genuinely moved. He had never seen him flat.

After class he caught Kabir's arm in the corridor.

"What happened?"

Kabir looked at him. Something moved in his expression — the effort of someone deciding how to carry a thing they have been carrying alone and finding it heavier than expected.

"The competition result," he said.

"You didn't win?"

"Someone else won." A pause. "With my project."

The group assembled at the amphitheater at lunch.

Not by announcement — by the specific gravity that pulls people together when something has gone wrong with one of their own. Meera arrived first after Aarav messaged her. Sanya came with her notebook already open, which meant she had been thinking since Aarav's message arrived and had already begun. Geet came because Sanya came and took one look at Kabir's face and sat down without saying a single word, which for Geet was an act of profound self-discipline.

Niel arrived last. He sat. He looked at Kabir.

"Tell me exactly what was submitted," he said. "Yours and his."

"I don't know what he submitted. I only know what the notice says. *Campus Unseen.* A documentary about college life." Kabir's voice was careful. Controlled. The voice of someone managing themselves very precisely. "Mine was called *The Campus, Nobody Shows You.* Also, a documentary. Also, about college life."

"Same subject."

"Same subject. Same approach. Same — " He stopped. "I haven't seen his. Maybe it's completely different. Maybe I'm wrong."

"You're not wrong," Niel said.

Everyone looked at him.

"I met Vikram in the first week," Niel said. "He approached me after class. Asked about research methods. Asked which projects I was working on." He paused. "He had the specific friendliness of someone building a list."

Silence.

"You knew?" Aarav said.

"I knew he was the kind of person who collected other people's work. I didn't know he had already acted." Niel looked at Kabir. "When did you submit?"

"Tuesday two weeks ago. Late. Eleven at night."

"From the media lab?"

"Yes."

Niel nodded slowly. The nod of someone whose calculation has just completed.

"We need to see his submission," he said.

Rohan arrived twenty minutes later.

He did not come from the direction of the classrooms or the hostel. He came from the administrative block — walking with that particular Rohan pace that gave nothing away and always seemed to be coming from somewhere it could not quite explain.

He sat at his end of the steps.

He looked at Kabir.

"I know about Vikram," he said.

The group went very still.

"How long?" Aarav said.

"Since last year." Rohan looked at his hands. "He did it to a third-year student in the previous batch. Design project. She reported it. The HOD took it to the principal. The principal took it to the board." He paused. "Vikram's father is on the board."

"Nothing happened," Sanya said. Not a question.

"The girl withdrew the complaint. She needed her degree. She needed her recommendation letter. She could not afford to fight a trustee's son for six months with no guarantee of winning."

The amphitheater was very quiet.

"You knew this," Aarav said. "All semester. You knew what he was capable of and you said nothing."

Rohan looked at him steadily. "I said nothing because knowing is not enough. I have known for a year. Knowing alone achieves nothing against a trustee connection. I needed — " He stopped. Chose the next word carefully. "Position."

"What does that mean?"

"It means I spent this semester making myself useful to the right people in the administration. Attending the right meetings. Being seen as aligned with the right interests." He looked at Aarav. "The marking scheme incident — that was part of it. I needed access to the administrative shared systems. I have it now."

Niel was watching Rohan with an expression of complete attention.

"You were building a case," Niel said.

"I was building access," Rohan said. "I needed a case to put in it." He looked at Kabir. "Now I have one."

Kabir stared at him. "You knew he might come after someone in this group?"

"I knew he would come after someone eventually. I did not know who." Something crossed Rohan's face — brief, honest, the closest he came to an apology. "I should have warned you to be more careful with your submissions. That is the one thing I got wrong."

Kabir looked at him for a long moment.

Then he nodded. Once. The specific nod of someone filing a thing away to process later when there is time.

"Okay," he said. "So, what do we do?"

Sanya had been writing since Rohan started talking.

She looked up from her notebook.

"We need three things," she said. With the calm efficiency of someone who has converted anger into action, which was Sanya's specific superpower. "One — a copy of Vikram's submission to compare against Kabir's original files. Two — evidence that Kabir's files were accessed without authorisation before his submission. Three — a channel to present this that the trustee connection cannot reach."

"The competition had external judges," Niel said. "Two of them. From outside the college."

"Can you reach them?"

"I can find them." He said it the way he said most things — simply, as a statement of fact rather than a boast.

"Rohan," Sanya said. "The administrative access — can you get Vikram's submission file?"

"Already have it," Rohan said.

He took out his phone. Showed her the screen.

Sanya looked at it. Then at Kabir. "Do you have your original files? Timestamped?"

"Everything. Every draft. Fourteen versions going back six weeks."

"Good." She closed her notebook. Opened it again to a fresh page. "Then we have a case."

Geet had been silent for the entire conversation.

This was — by any measure — the longest Geet had been silent since joining the group. She had been sitting very still with her hands in her lap and an expression that was completely uncharacteristic. Not chaos. Not movement. Just — thinking.

"Geet," Sanya said, noticing. "Are you alright?"

"The printer," Geet said.

Everyone looked at her.

"Three weeks ago. I went to the media lab for the printer. There was a person there." She looked at Kabir. "Tall. Nice watch. He was at a computer that wasn't his. I remember thinking it was strange and then I found the printer and I forgot about it." She swallowed. "I think it was him. I think I was there. I think I saw it."

The amphitheater absorbed this.

"You're a witness," Niel said quietly.

Geet looked at him. "I didn't know I was witnessing anything."

"You never do," he said. "That's what makes it count."

Niel found the external judges in four hours.

This was the kind of thing Niel did without announcing he was going to do it — he simply disappeared into whatever focused state he operated in when something needed to be solved, and emerged with the answer. Two judges. One a media professional from Mumbai. One an academic from a Pune university with no extra details.

He wrote to both of them that evening.

Not emotionally. Not dramatically. With the precise, documented, professionally structured communication of someone who knew that the strength of a case was in its evidence not its feeling.

He attached Kabir's original files with timestamps. He attached Rohan's copy of Vikram's submission. He attached a written account from Geet — which Sanya had helped her write with careful specificity — describing what she had seen in the media lab and when.

He sent it.

Then he closed his laptop.

"Now we wait," he said.

"How long?" Aarav asked.

"As long as it takes." He looked at Aarav. "But not long. People who care about the integrity of their own judgements move quickly when that integrity is questioned."

Kabir was on the hostel terrace when Aarav found him that night.

Same ledge. Same city. Different weight in the air.

He was not crying. He was not angry. He was doing something quieter and harder — he was sitting with the specific pain of having made something genuinely his and having it taken, and trying to decide whether that taking diminished the thing itself.

"It was good," Aarav said. Sitting beside him. "Whatever happens. It was good work."

"I know," Kabir said. And the way he said it — without deflection, without a joke to cushion it — was its own kind of growth. "That's the thing. I know it was good. He took it because it was good." A pause. "That's almost funny."

"Almost."

"Venky Sir would probably say something about this. Something that makes it make sense." Kabir looked at the sky. "What do you think he'd say?"

Aarav thought about it honestly.

"I think he'd say that what was made cannot be unmade. That the work is yours regardless of whose name is on it. That originality lives in the maker not the submission portal." He paused. "And then he'd tell you to stop being sentimental and think about what happens next."

Kabir was quiet for a moment.

Then — small, real, the first one in two days — a smile.

"Yeah," he said. "That sounds right."

They sat together on the ledge. The city below them doing its city things. The campus behind them doing its campus things.

"Aarav," Kabir said.

"Yeah."

"Whatever happens with the judges — I'm going to make another one. A better one." He looked at the skyline. "He can have that one. I'll make ten more."

Aarav looked at him.

This — right here — was who Kabir actually was underneath the punchlines. Not just the funny one. Not just the light of the group. Someone with a spine made of something very quietly strong.

"I know you will," Aarav said.

Venky Sir called Aarav to his office the next morning.

He did not explain how he knew. He simply knew — the way he always knew, operating on some frequency of attention that picked up what ordinary observation missed.

He poured chai. Slid one cup across.

"Vikram Nair," he said.

Aarav looked at him.

"I know the name," Venky Sir said quietly. He looked at his cup. "I know what he did last year. I know what I was unable to do about it." He paused — a long one, carrying weight. "I have been carrying that particular failure for twelve months."

"We're handling it," Aarav said.

"I know you are." Venky Sir looked at him. "That is not why I called you here." He set his cup down. "I called you here to tell you one thing." He looked at Aarav with that gaze — the one that went all the way through. "Do it cleanly. Whatever you do — do it in a way you can stand behind completely. No grey. No shortcuts. Not because Vikram deserves your integrity. Because Kabir does."

The office was quiet.

"Evidence," Aarav said. "External judges. Nothing else."

Venky Sir picked up his chai.

"Good," he said.

He turned back to his papers.

Aarav stood to leave.

"Sir," he said.

Venky Sir looked up.

"We've got this one."

Venky Sir held his gaze for a moment.

Something moved in his expression. Not just pride. Relief. The specific relief of a second chance arriving before it was too late.

"I know," he said softly.

"Good," said Aarav.

He left.

Chapter 11: Hearts & Hustle

November in Pune arrives like a quiet agreement between the city and the weather.

The heat of October steps back. The air becomes something you actually want to breathe — cooler, cleaner, carrying the particular smell of wet leaves and early morning mist off the Ghats. The campus in November had a specific quality that the group had come to associate with the feeling of things getting serious — not in a heavy way, but in the way of a story reaching the part where all the pieces that have been moving start to find their places.

Exams were six weeks away.

The college fest — Resonance, the annual two-day event that the cultural committee had been planning since August — was in three.

And everything was happening at once, which was, as Kabir observed with the authority of someone who had studied chaos closely for several years, simply what final semesters did. They collapsed all the important things into the same window and watched you try to hold them all.

Kabir called his father on a Tuesday.

He did it from the hostel terrace — the same spot where he and Aarav had talked, which felt right. He sat on the water tank ledge with his phone in his hand for four minutes before dialling, which was the closest Kabir ever came to hesitation.

His father answered on the second ring.

The conversation lasted forty minutes. Kabir had not planned a speech — he had learned, partly from watching Aarav at the amphitheater, that speeches gave you a structure to hide inside when the real thing required open ground.

So, he simply said it.

He said he respected the business. He said he understood what his father had built, what his grandfather had started, what the family name meant in Ulhasnagar. He said none of that was lost on him and none of it was small.

And then he said: I have something I need to build too. Something that is mine the way the business is yours. And I need to try it, Papa. Not after I've done the safe thing first. Now, while I'm still the person who believes I can.

The line was quiet for a moment.

His father said: I need time to think.

Kabir said: I know, Papa. Take it.

He hung up.

He sat on the ledge for a while. The Pune skyline was doing its Tuesday morning thing — ordinary, unhurried, completely indifferent to the size of what had just happened.

He felt lighter than he had in months.

Not because it was resolved. It wasn't resolved. His father had said nothing definitive, no blessing, no endorsement. The conversation had produced no answers.

But it had produced honesty. And honesty, Kabir was discovering, had its own kind of weight that worked in the opposite direction — instead of pressing down, it lifted.

He pulled out his phone and typed a message to Aarav: *Did it.*

Aarav replied in twelve seconds: *And?*

He needs time.

That's not a no.

I know, Kabir typed. Then, after a moment: Venky Sir was right. It's just courage.

Aarav sent back a single word: *Always.*

Geet's contribution to Resonance was, by any measure, the most complicated administrative achievement of the semester.

She had signed up to coordinate stage bookings for the two-day event — which was a reasonable task for a reasonably organised person, which Geet was not, but which she approached with such complete sincerity that the cultural committee had agreed on the strength of her enthusiasm alone.

The problem emerged four days before the festival when Geet, cross-referencing her booking spreadsheet with the confirmed performer list, discovered that she had allocated two different groups to the main stage for the same ninety-minute slot on day one.

She stared at this discovery for a long time.

Then she opened a new tab and looked at it again, in case it had changed.

It had not changed.

She went to Sanya.

Sanya looked at the spreadsheet. Then at Geet. Then back at the spreadsheet with the expression of someone completing an internal calculation that ended in a very large number.

"Both groups are confirmed?" she said.

"Both groups are confirmed."

"And neither can be moved?"

"The dance group has a choreographer coming from Mumbai who cannot change dates. The band has a sound engineer who is only available that evening." Geet paused. "I may have created an impossible situation."

"You definitely created an impossible situation."

"Can you tell me a way it isn't impossible?"

Sanya looked at the spreadsheet for another moment.

"What if," she said slowly, "they perform together?"

Geet looked at her.

"The band provides live music. The dance group performs to it. Neither group loses their slot — they share it." Sanya turned the laptop toward Geet. "It would require them to collaborate in four days, which is tight, but—"

"It would be extraordinary," Geet said. Her eyes had gone bright.

"It would be chaotic."

"Chaotic is my speciality."

"That," Sanya said, "is unfortunately true."

The collaboration happened.

It happened with the specific magic of things that are improvised under pressure by people who are good at what they do. The band — four postgrad students who had been playing together for two years — spent two evenings learning the dance group's timings. The dance group spent the same evenings learning to feel the music rather than follow a fixed recording.

On the evening of Resonance's first day, the main stage hosted something that nobody had planned and everybody remembered.

Live music and live dance, unrehearsed enough to be surprising, rehearsed enough to be beautiful. The audience

— students, faculty, a handful of parents — went from curious to absorbed to on their feet within twenty minutes.

At the back of the auditorium, Geet stood next to Sanya watching it happen.

"I did this," Geet said quietly.

"You did this by accident," Sanya said.

"The best things happen by accident."

Sanya looked at her sideways. Then at the stage. Then she smiled — genuinely, fully — and said nothing.

Kabir, three rows from the front, turned around to find the group. When he found Geet at the back, he pointed at her and mouthed: *You.*

Geet pointed back at herself with an expression of complete innocence. Nodded.

Kabir shook his head, laughing.

Niel's scholarship letter arrived on the second day of Resonance.

The fellowship shortlist discussions had taken over the postgrad corridors that week.

Every second conversation involved rankings, recommendations, interviews, or somebody's cousin who "knew someone on the panel."

Sanya was scrolling through shortlisted profiles when she stopped briefly. "Hmm."

Kabir looked up immediately. "That is never a safe sound. What happened?"

"There's a Mumbai candidate everyone keeps mentioning." Sanya Said.

"Another LinkedIn philosopher?" Kabir asked furiously.

"Worse," Sanya said. "Apparently competent."

That got Niel's attention. "Who?"

"Shiv Malhotra."

Even Niel looked mildly thoughtful at the name.

Aarav frowned. "Should I know him?"

"Rich family," Sanya said casually. "Brilliant. Short-tempered. Apparently impossible to out-argue."

Kabir leaned back dramatically. "Fantastic. I already dislike him."

Niel read it in the morning, alone in his room, before coming to the festival. He sat with it for a long time.

The scholarship was real. A two-year research programme. Fully funded. Starting the following academic year.

He folded the letter. Put it in his bag. Came to the festival.

He said nothing about it.

He watched the events. He ate vada pav with Kabir. He listened to Geet explain, in great detail, how the previous evening's performance had been a strategic decision rather than a happy accident. He sat with the group in the comfortable way he had come to sit with this group — present, quiet, genuinely there.

At the end of the day, as the campus began its slow wind-down, he went to Venky Sir's office.

He put the letter on the desk without saying anything.

Venky Sir read it. His expression did not change dramatically. But something in it — some quality of attention — sharpened.

He looked up at Niel. "What is stopping you?" he said.

"Nothing," Niel said.

"Then why are you here?"

Niel thought about it honestly. "I wanted someone to know," he said. "Before I decided. I wanted — " He paused, finding the precise word. "Witness."

Venky Sir was quiet for a moment.

He looked at the letter again.

Then he slid it back across the desk.

"Take it," he said. "Go."

Niel picked up the letter.

"Will you?" he said. It was a small question, the kind that contains a larger one.

Venky Sir understood the larger one.

"I'll be here," he said simply. "That's not going anywhere."

Niel nodded.

He stood to leave.

"Niel," Venky Sir said.

He turned.

Venky Sir looked at him — with something that was not a teacher looking at a student, or not only that. Something older and quieter.

"Make it matter," he said.

Niel held that. "Yes sir," he said and left.

Venky Sir sat in the office for a while after. He did not pick up his chai. He looked at the space where Niel had been sitting with an expression that contained several things — pride, something wistful, the particular look of a person who sees a younger version of their own best qualities going out into the world and knows they have done their part.

He thought about a question Niel had asked him, early in the semester, in the corridor: *The sky performs before it commits.*

He thought about Radha.

Kabir performed that evening.

Not as the funny one. Not as the person who kept everyone entertained because it was easier than being serious. He performed as himself — the version underneath, the one only the terrace had seen.

He told stories. About the campus. About the chai tapri at seven in the morning. About the library at midnight. About the specific way this place looked in the rain. He did not have a camera this time. Just himself and the microphone and four hundred people in a dark auditorium.

He made them laugh. He made them quiet. He made them feel something about a place they lived in every day and had perhaps stopped actually seeing.

At the back of the auditorium, Aarav stood next to Meera.

She was watching Kabir with an expression that was entirely without performance — just genuine, full, proud.

Aarav watched her watch him.

Then he watched Kabir.

The person on that stage — completely himself, completely at ease, making a room feel things on purpose — was the person Kabir had always been. He had just been waiting for permission to show up as him.

The audience responded the way audiences respond to the true thing.

They forgot to be an audience. They just felt it.

The reply from the first judge came on the morning of Resonance.

Niel read it once. Then walked directly to where Aarav was standing near the amphitheater and handed him his phone without a word.

Aarav read it.

The judge had reviewed both submissions overnight. His email was four paragraphs long and precise in the way of someone who took the integrity of their own judgement very seriously. He had identified seventeen specific points of duplication. He had copied the second judge. He had notified the competition secretariat.

He had also — in the final paragraph, almost as an aside — written something about the original work itself. About its honesty. Its specific vision. The quality of attention it brought to an ordinary subject.

Aarav looked up from the phone.

"Kabir needs to read this," he said.

"Not yet," Niel said. He took his phone back. "Let him perform tonight. Let him have that. The letter comes after."

Aarav looked at him.

"He needs to know he is still the person who made it," Niel said quietly. "Before he knows what happens to the person who stole it."

Aarav nodded.

On the second evening of Resonance, a screen appeared in the smaller seminar room beside the main auditorium.

No announcement. No poster. No entry in the official programme. Just a handwritten sheet of paper taped to the door that said:

The Campus, Nobody Shows You. 22 minutes. Come in if you want.

Kabir had booked the room three days ago. Before the judges had responded. Before the letter. Before any of it was resolved. He had booked it because he had decided — sitting on the terrace with Aarav, the city spread out below them — that the film existed and the film was his and nobody's name on a competition portal changed either of those facts.

He had not told anyone. Not even Aarav.

At seven-fifteen the room had eleven people in it.

By seven-twenty it had thirty.

By seven twenty-five, people were sitting on the floor, leaning against the back wall, standing in the doorway.

Someone had propped the door open. People in the corridor were watching from outside.

Nobody had announced anything. The campus had simply done what campuses do — word moved from person to person in the specific fast quiet way of something genuinely worth seeing.

Kabir sat at the back.

He had not introduced the film. He had not stood at the front and explained what it was or why he had made it. He had simply connected his laptop to the projector, pressed play, and sat down in the last row.

The film opened with the chai tapri.

Five-forty-five in the morning. The sky not fully light yet. The tapri owner — old man, always there before anyone else — setting out glasses with the unhurried precision of someone who had done this ten thousand times and intended to do it ten thousand more. Steam rising. The first student of the day arriving, bag half-open, hair uncombed, buying chai with the automatic movement of someone still mostly asleep.

No narration. Just the sound of the morning. The clink of glass. The hiss of the gas flame. A bird somewhere making its case for the day.

The room was completely quiet.

The film moved through the campus the way a good eye moves — not rushing, not performing, just looking. Honestly and with attention.

The library at eleven at night. Four students at one table, all facing different directions, all in the private country of their own concentration. One asleep. One mouthing words silently. One staring at the ceiling with the expression of someone waiting for an idea to arrive and not being sure it would.

The notice board. Hands stopping at it — dozens of different hands, over different days, reaching out to read or touch or pin something. Nobody's face. Just hands and paper and the specific gesture of someone looking for something that matters.

The amphitheater steps in the rain. Empty. The water moving across the stone in small rivers. Then one student arriving, sitting down anyway, opening a book, reading in the rain with the complete serenity of someone who had decided the weather was not their problem.

The corridor outside the staffroom on a Thursday afternoon — a shot held for almost a minute. Nothing happening. Just the light changing. A door opening and closing somewhere off-camera. Footsteps passing. The campus breathing.

Halfway through, Kabir looked at the room.

He had expected — he was not sure what he had expected. Restlessness maybe. The polite attention people gave things they were not fully interested in. Phones emerging.

What he saw instead was forty people watching their own life and recognising it.

Not with nostalgia — they were still inside it; this was not memory yet. With something rarer. The specific feeling of seeing clearly a thing you are normally too close to see at all.

A girl in the third row had her hand over her mouth.

A group of four boys who had come in together — the kind of boys who came to things in groups and made noise about it — were sitting completely still and completely separate, each inside their own private response.

At the back of the room, standing in the doorway because there was no more floor space, Aarav watched.

He had found out twenty minutes ago. Meera had seen the handwritten sign and texted him one word: *Come.*

He stood in the doorway and watched the film and watched the room watching the film and felt something that he would not have been able to name precisely but which was in the neighbourhood of: *this is why.*

This is why Kabir needed the year. This is why the dream was real. Not because it was commercially viable or strategically sound or any of the things fathers reasonably worried about. Because forty people were sitting in a seminar room on a festival evening watching their own ordinary campus life and feeling something true about it.

That was the reason.

The film ended the way it had begun. The chai tapri. Evening this time. The owner wiping down the counter with the same unhurried precision as the opening. The last student of the day buying the last chai. Steam rising. The gas flame turned off. The owner picking up his bag. Looking back once at the tapri — not sentimentally, just checking — and walking away.

Darkness.

The projector went white.

The room was silent for a long moment.

Then someone started clapping. Not Geet — someone in the middle of the room, someone Kabir didn't know, a second-year student he had never spoken to. Then the rest of the room joined. Not the polite end-of-presentation kind. The other kind. The kind that means something was felt and the only available response is this.

Kabir sat at the back of the room and looked at his hands.

He had made this.

Vikram had put his name on a stolen version of it. The judges had found seventeen points of duplication. None of that had touched the film itself. The film was exactly what it had always been — twenty-two minutes of honest attention paid to a place and the people inside it.

Nobody could submit that as their own.

It was too completely his.

Niel appeared beside him.

He had come in ten minutes before the end and found the last available patch of floor space near the back wall. He sat down next to Kabir without saying anything. Watched the final minutes.

Now, in the silence after, he looked at the screen.

"You should have submitted this to something bigger than a college competition," he said.

Kabir looked at him. "I did submit it to a college competition."

"I know. Submit it somewhere bigger next."

Kabir was quiet for a moment.

"Yeah," he said. "I think I will."

They found Geet outside, in the corridor.

She had watched from the doorway — standing on her toes to see over people's heads — and had apparently been crying for the last eight minutes, which she was now dealing with by pretending she had something in both eyes simultaneously.

"Both eyes," Kabir said.

"Allergies," Geet said.

"To what?"

"Good filmmaking apparently."

Kabir looked at her.

She looked back at him with her actual expression — the one underneath the chaos, the one that was simply genuine and warm and entirely without performance.

"It was really good, Kabir," she said. "Really, actually, properly good."

He nodded.

He did not deflect it. Did not make a joke. Did not redirect.

He just said: "Thank you."

And meant it completely.

That was the evening the group understood — each of them separately, in their own way — that Kabir was not the funny one.

He was the one who paid attention. Who noticed the chai tapri at five-forty-five and the student reading in the rain and the hands at the notice board and the library at midnight.

Who looked at the ordinary campus life around him and saw something worth showing.

The funny was just how he carried it until the world was ready to see it.

The evening of the second day settled over the campus the way good evenings do — gradually, warmly, without announcement.

The festival was winding down. The stage was quiet. Students moved in loose groups across the courtyard, carrying the particular pleasant tiredness of two days well spent.

The group gathered at the amphitheater. All of them — Aarav, Meera, Kabir, Sanya, Geet, Niel, and at the far end, Rohan. Seven people in their spot. The city glowing beyond the campus walls.

Kabir had acquired chai for everyone through means he declined to specify. Geet was still wearing her festival kurta. Sanya had her notebook open but was not writing in it — just holding it, the way you hold familiar things.

"Good two days," Kabir said.

"Exceptional two days," Geet corrected.

"Your definition of exceptional involves accidentally creating the best performance of the festival."

"That's what exceptional means," Geet said with complete dignity.

Laughter moved around the group.

Aarav and Meera were sitting close — the way they had been sitting since the amphitheater Thursday, which was to say naturally, without announcement, close enough that their arms touched. Nobody made a point of it. It had simply become part of the landscape of the group, like Kabir's punchlines and Sanya's notebook and Niel's book.

Rohan and Niel both looked at the city. Neither said anything. Something in the evening air had the quality of a held breath — not tense, but full. The specific feeling of a semester that has moved through enough things to have earned its rest.

Then Kabir said, into the quiet: "Can I say something without it being a joke?"

Everyone looked at him.

"This year," he said. He stopped. Started again. "This group." He looked around at all of them — genuinely, without the performance layer that usually sat between Kabir and his deepest feelings. "I don't know what I would have done without it. Any of it." He looked at Aarav. "Any of you."

Silence.

Geet, who was constitutionally unable to tolerate emotional silences without doing something about them, started to clap.

Sanya caught her hand gently. "Not this time," she said softly.

Geet stopped. Nodded.

They sat with it instead. Let it be what it was. Kabir's honest thing, offered without deflection, received without deflection.

It was one of the quietest, most complete moments the group had ever shared.

Later, walking back across the campus, Aarav and Meera fell behind the group the way they did now — naturally, without planning, because some gravity had reoriented between them and this was simply where they ended up.

The campus at night had its specific beauty — the library lights, the courtyard lamps, the distant sound of the city, the smell of dust and old stone and whatever the canteen had been making all evening.

They walked without talking for a bit.

Then Meera said: "Do you think we'll remember all of it?"

Aarav thought about the question honestly. "Not all of it," he said. "But the important parts. The parts that changed something."

"Like what?"

"The gate on the first day. The visarjan. The amphitheater." He glanced at her. "The dupatta."

She laughed softly. "You know about the dupatta?"

"You just told me, when you—" He stopped. "Oh. You told me that night. I mean the fact of it. Not what it meant to you."

"And what do you think it meant to me?" she said.

She was looking at him with that clear, direct gaze. No game in it. Just honest.

"I think," Aarav said, "it meant that you already knew. Before you let yourself know."

She was quiet for a step.

"Yes," she said. "That's exactly what it meant."

They walked on. Close. Unhurried. The campus quiet around them. The city doing its city things on the other side of the wall.

No grand moment. No dramatic pause.

Just two people walking together through the place that had made them who they were, which was its own kind of everything.

Chapter 12: The Morning After the Night Before

The morning arrived like mornings do after great evenings — with the mild surprise of ordinary things being exactly where you left them.

The campus looked the same. The pigeons were arguing on the library roof again. The security guard was in his chair with his specific expression of magnificent indifference. The chai tapri was producing its constant ribbon of steam — that sweet smell of elaichi and ginger that meant the day had properly started.

Everything was the same.

Everything was different.

Aarav and Meera walked to the postgrad block together.

Not hand in hand. Not dramatically. Simply together, in the easy side-by-side way that was both identical to how they had walked before and completely transformed by the fact of what they now knew about each other. The conversation was about ordinary things — an assignment deadline, whether the canteen pohe was going to be good today, what Geet would probably do next.

An entirely unremarkable conversation.

Which was, Aarav thought, the most remarkable thing about it. That it was unremarkable. That the truest version of them was this — easy, ordinary, themselves.

They went to class.

The group assembled at the tapri at break time with the natural timing of people whose internal clocks had been synchronised by three years of shared life.

Kabir arrived first, which was unusual enough that Sanya noted it in her notebook under *anomalies.* He had two cutting chai already in hand and an expression of settled happiness that was different from his usual performance — deeper, less for the room.

He looked at Aarav and Meera arriving together.

He pointed at them. "Finally," he said. "I had a speech prepared. I've been carrying it since September."

"You did not have a speech," Aarav said.

"I had the outline of a speech. The emotional core. I was going to improvise the rest."

"That's not a speech," Meera said. "That's a feeling."

Kabir considered this. "Fine. I had a feeling. I've been carrying it since September." He handed them their chais. "You're welcome."

Sanya arrived, looked at them both, and simply smiled — the full one, the real one that she didn't give out freely and which meant more because of it.

Geet arrived having come from the wrong direction again. She stopped when she read the room.

"Wait," she said. She looked at Aarav. She looked at Meera. She looked at Kabir's expression. She looked at Sanya's smile.

"Wait," she said again.

"Geet—" Sanya began.

"SINCE WHEN?" Geet said.

Everyone within earshot turned to look.

"Since last week," Meera said quietly.

"Last WEEK?" Geet looked personally betrayed. "I have been sitting next to Sanya for WEEKS and nobody — " She turned to Sanya. "You knew."

"I knew," Sanya said.

"You didn't TELL me."

"It wasn't mine to tell."

Geet stared at her. Then she looked at Aarav and Meera. Then something in her expression softened entirely — the outrage dissolving into something genuine and warm.

"Okay," she said. She picked up her chai. "Okay. This is good. This is actually very good."

She raised her cup.

"To finally," she said.

Kabir raised his immediately. "To finally."

Sanya raised hers. A smile.

Aarav and Meera looked at each other.

He raised his cup. She raised hers.

They drank.

Niel arrived two minutes later, saw the group in their slightly ceremonial state, and received the information from Kabir in approximately twelve words.

He looked at Aarav.

He gave one quiet nod — the kind that contained everything: *I know. I told you. Good.*

That was it. No ceremony. No performance.

Aarav gave one quiet nod back.

Between two people who communicated efficiently, this was a complete conversation.

Rohan heard from nobody.

He simply appeared at the amphitheater that afternoon, as he always did, and looked at Aarav and Meera sitting close in the way that was now natural between them.

He said nothing.

He looked back at his phone.

But Aarav, watching from the corner of his eye, saw it — brief, small, real.

Rohan smiled.

Not the performed kind. Not the grey kind. Just a smile. Quiet and private and directed at nobody in particular.

Gone in a second.

Aarav filed it away.

Gray is not the whole story, he thought. It never was.

The letter arrived on Thursday.

Not digitally. Printed. In an envelope addressed to Kabir by name, left at the postgrad department office by a courier who had no idea what he was carrying.

Kabir found it in his pigeonhole at eleven in the morning. He looked at the return address. Read it twice. Put it in his bag without opening it and carried it for four hours before he could make himself sit down with it.

He went to the terrace.

He sat on the ledge — the same spot, always the same spot — and opened it.

It was from the first external judge. One page. Typed. The kind of letter that does not waste words because every word has been chosen.

He read it once.

He read it again.

Then he sat very still for a long moment with the paper in both hands and the Pune skyline doing its Thursday afternoon thing completely indifferent to what was happening on this particular terrace.

The letter said many things. It said what had been found and what had been decided and what the formal outcome of the review was. It said these things clearly and without drama.

And then — in the final paragraph, the one Niel had seen first and had known needed to wait until now — it said this:

The original work demonstrates a quality of observation that is rare in student submissions and not uncommon in professional ones. The filmmaker has a genuine eye. I would encourage him strongly to continue.

Kabir read that paragraph four times.

Genuine eye.

He folded the letter carefully. Put it back in the envelope. Put the envelope in his bag.

He looked at the city.

He thought about his father. About one year of trust and what it meant to have something real — not a prize, not a result, not a rank — but a paragraph from someone who had no reason to say it except that it was true.

He took out his phone.

He called his father.

It rang twice.

"Papa," he said. His voice was steady. "I have something to tell you."

That evening, at the amphitheater, Kabir arrived last.

He sat down. Looked at the group. All of them watching him with the specific attention of people who already knew and were waiting for him to be ready.

He took out the envelope.

He did not read it aloud. He passed it to Aarav. Aarav read it and passed it to Meera. Meera to Sanya. Sanya to Geet. Geet to Niel. Niel — who had already read it — held it for a moment and passed it to Rohan.

Rohan read it.

He folded it. Handed it back to Kabir.

Said nothing.

But he nodded — once, slow, the certain kind.

That was enough.

Geet started clapping.

Nobody stopped her.

That evening, Venky Sir stood at the corridor window with his chai.

The campus below was doing its November evening things — students crossing the courtyard, the tapri busy, a group at the amphitheater steps. He could see them from here. All seven of them, in their spot, in the light that fell across the campus at this particular hour.

He watched for a moment.

He saw Aarav and Meera. He saw Kabir making everyone laugh. He saw Sanya with her notebook and her real smile. He saw Geet gesturing at something with great enthusiasm. He saw Niel at the edge — present, quiet, the scholarship letter folded in his bag. He saw Rohan at the far end, slightly apart, as always.

He saw all of them.

He thought about the first day he had seen Aarav — furious and betrayed and standing outside the Placement Office with nowhere to put his anger. He thought about Kabir making everyone laugh from behind a wall of carefully maintained lightness. He thought about Meera finding herself in a music room, alone at a piano. He thought about Sanya and her colour-coded notebook that had always been, at its heart, a way of making the world feel manageable.

He thought about Niel. The corridor. *The sky performs before it commits.*

Venky sir then thought about Radha.

He did not feel sad about Radha tonight. That particular feeling had a season, and tonight was not its season. Tonight he felt something simpler — the quiet fullness of a person who has put good things into the world and can see them from a window.

He raised his chai cup.

Not to anyone in particular.

Just — to it. All of it.

Then he turned from the window and went back to his desk.

Later that evening, Kabir sat on the hostel terrace again. Alone this time. His phone lit up with a message.

His father.

He opened it.

I spoke to your mother. Come home this weekend. We will talk properly.

Kabir read it three times.

Then he put his phone face-down on the ledge and looked at the Pune sky — the city that had made him, in the last four years, into someone he actually recognised when he looked in the mirror.

He thought about Venky Sir's question.

If failure was not possible, what would you do?

He already knew the answer. He had always known it. The question had just given him permission to say it out loud.

He picked up his phone and replied: *I'll be there.*

He put the phone away.

He looked at the sky for a while.

Then, because he was Kabir and this was fundamentally who he was, he said aloud to nobody:

"Okay, universe. Let's see what you've got."

The last Friday of November arrived with the particular quality of a day that doesn't know it's significant.

The group was at FC Road. All seven of them — Geet had simply been there from the beginning now, which was how the group had quietly expanded without a meeting or a vote or anyone noticing the exact moment it happened. She was simply part of it, the way Niel was part of it, the way Rohan was part of it in his particular peripheral way.

Vada pav. Chai. The FC Road evening in full expression — the bookshops and the noise and the city going about the specific business of being Pune.

Kabir was telling a story about the hostel warden and a missing ceiling fan that grew more elaborate with each sentence. Geet was adding sound effects. Sanya was writing something in her notebook and laughing at the same time, which was a coordination achievement. Niel was listening with the quality of attention that meant he was filing it for later. Rohan had, unusually, moved slightly closer to the group — not inside it exactly, but less at the edge than usual.

And Aarav and Meera were at the low wall outside the nameless bookshop, slightly apart from the group the way they often were now — not separated from it, just in their own orbit within it.

Meera was reading something on her phone. Aarav was watching the road.

"What are you thinking about?" she asked without looking up.

"The gate," he said.

She looked up. "The campus gate?"

"First day. Standing outside it." He looked at the FC Road evening around them. "I thought — something is beginning. I just didn't know what."

Meera looked at him.

"And now?"

He considered it. Looked at the group — Kabir at full volume, Geet contributing enthusiastically, Sanya laughing, Niel quiet and present, Rohan almost smiling. Looked at the city. Looked at her.

"Now I know," he said simply.

A notification flashed briefly on Aarav's phone.

He checked it absentmindedly at first.

Then read it again.

Meera noticed the shift in his expression immediately.

"What happened?"

Aarav locked the screen instinctively. "Nothing."

She kept looking at him.

After a few seconds, he exhaled softly. "Placement shortlist."

"That's good, right?"

"Yeah," he said.

But something in his voice carried the strange weight of a person realizing that life had finally started moving faster than comfort.

She held his gaze for a moment.

Then she leaned her head on his shoulder.

Just that. No grand gesture. The FC Road evening moved around them — noisy and warm and indifferent and wonderful — and she rested her head on his shoulder and he stayed still, and the city did what cities do, which is continue being alive in every direction all at once.

Somewhere across the city, in his small apartment near the college, Venky Sir sat at his desk after dinner.

The apartment was the way it had always been — books on every surface, a small window that looked at a narrow street, the photograph on the desk near the lamp.

Radha.

She was smiling in the photograph — the genuine kind, the kind that happened in the middle of something rather than for the camera. She was young in it. They both had been.

He looked at it for a while. He thought about what he had told Meera: The heart is not confused. It knows exactly what it wants. It is the mind that keeps asking for proof.

He had meant it when he said it. He still meant it.

He thought about his students — all of them, across all the years, the ones who had sat in that chair and worked things out slowly with his bad tea and his deliberate questions. He thought about the ones who had come back years later and said *that conversation changed something.* He thought about the ones he never heard from again, who he hoped had gone on to lives that fit them properly.

He thought about Niel. *Make it matter.*

He turned off the lamp. He sat in the dark for a moment — not sadly, just quietly — in the specific way of a person who has made peace with the shape of his life and found it, on most evenings, to be a good shape.

He thought: Some stories don't end. They just get better.

He went to bed.

Epilogue: One More Beginning

The December arrived.

Exams came and were survived in the specific way exams always are — badly, then adequately, then better than expected. The postgrad semester closed with the particular mix of relief and mild disbelief that follows any sustained period of effort.

Grades were posted. The batch celebrated. Kabir announced that his father had agreed to give him one year to pursue media — *one year, then we talk again* — which Kabir had accepted as the most reasonable thing he had ever been offered. Geet passed all her papers, including the one she had been certain she had failed, and responded to this news by buying the chai tapri owner a plant. A large one. In a pot that said *thank you for existing* on it.

The plant remains there to this day.

Niel accepted the scholarship. He told the group on the last day of semester at the amphitheater, simply and without drama, and the group received it with the particular warmth of people who are genuinely happy for someone rather than performing happiness.

"You'll come back," Kabir said.

"Yes," Niel said.

"Promise."

Niel looked at him. "Yes," he said again.

Rohan, at the end of the steps, said nothing. But he nodded once — the slow, certain kind.

On the last day before the winter break, Aarav found himself at the campus gate.

He was not sure how he had ended up there. He had been heading to the tapri and had taken a longer route without deciding to. And then he was at the gate, looking at the notice board.

The same one. Sun-bleached. Slightly crooked. Different flyers now, same position.

He thought about the first day of *Campus Crossroads* — standing on the other side of this gate, full of something he couldn't name. He thought about every version of the campus he had known since then. The corruption he had fought. The friendships that had broken and repaired themselves. The election. The leadership. The slow, patient arrival of love. The gate at the beginning of this year, stepping through and thinking: *like coming home.*

He heard footsteps behind him.

He turned.

Meera, Kabir, Sanya, Geet. All four of them, having followed him apparently without coordination, in the way people who know each other well often end up in the same direction.

Niel appeared from the library side. Rohan materialised from wherever Rohan materialised from.

All seven of them at the gate.

Looking at it together.

Nobody said anything for a moment.

Then Kabir said, with perfect timing and the exact right amount of feeling: "Same gate."

"Different people," Meera said.

Sanya looked at the notice board. "Better people," she said quietly.

Geet raised her hand. "I'm new here so I can't comment on the before. But the current version is excellent."

Laughter. The warm kind.

Aarav looked at the gate. Then at the campus behind it. Then at the city beyond the wall.

Then at the people beside him. He thought about Venky Sir's window. The raised chai cup on the first day. *We'll continue this.*

They would continue this.

Whatever came next — the second year, the real world, the futures they couldn't see yet — they would continue this.

He turned from the gate.

Across the courtyard, on the other side of the campus, a new student was standing at the notice board. Young. Slightly lost. Looking at the flyers with the expression of someone at the beginning of something enormous.

The same expression they had all worn once.

Somewhere in the postgrad block, a window was lit. A desk lamp. A chai cup sending up its ribbon of steam.

Venky Sir, at his desk, working late.

Still here. Always here.

The gate behind them. The campus ahead. The city all around.

Some stories don't end.

They just get better.

Three days after the letter arrived, a phone call was made.

Not by a student. Not by a judge. Not by anyone whose name appeared in any complaint or document or formal review.

By a man in an office on the third floor of a building whose name was on the college's founding trust deed.

He made one call.

To someone who owed him a favour.

About the postgrad programme.

About the students who had made the last month very inconvenient for his family.

He spoke for four minutes.

He hung up.

He straightened his cufflinks.

Outside his window, Pune went about its evening — loud and warm and completely unaware.

The campus was quiet.

For now.

Some storms announce themselves loudly.

This one didn't.

THE END

Beyond Grades and Gossips: Hearts & Hustle

Book 2

www.ingramcontent.com/pod-product-compliance
Lightning Source LLC
LaVergne TN
LVHW090610110826
845146LV00001B/326

* 9 7 8 9 3 5 8 9 0 1 0 7 8 *